# Mysteries of Africa

# Mysteries of Africa

*Eugene Schleh, editor*

Bowling Green State University Popular Press
Bowling Green, OH 43403

# Contents

# Introduction

Some readers might wonder why one would bother to read popular literature such as crime fiction to learn about Africa. It might be entertaining, but wouldn't the time be better spent reading political pamphlets or history books? After all, isn't popular literature, by its very nature, designed to sell widely, and must therefore consist largely of distortions rather than representations of reality? While it may contain some truths, aren't these truths bent to fit the expectations of a mass audience?

Undeniably, some of it is. But literature may be both insightful and entertaining, truthful and captivating, and a wholesale denigration of the value of popular literature is, itself, blind to some of the truths of history.

Consider some of the works that are now regarded as classics and considered worthy of inclusion in the curriculum of any university. British literature provides some striking examples. The bulk of England's literature from the medieval period is popular literature. The fact that Chaucer's *Canterbury Tales* survive in eighty-four manuscripts, all of them later than his time, attests to their popularity. The plays of Shakespeare endured, in part, because they appealed to groundlings as well as aristocrats. The novels of Henry Fielding, Samuel Richardson, Tobias Smollett, Laurence Sterne, Sir Walter Scott, and Charles Dickens all had widespread popularity in their time and have all achieved a respectable old age today. And scholars read Fielding's *Amelia*, for instance, to learn about conditions of prison life in 18th Century England, for Fielding the novelist/magistrate brought it to dramatic life in those pages, as Smollett did the grim and degrading lot of English seamen. Dickens is considered a reliable and important source for learning about social conditions in Victorian England, and who better than

1

Jane Austen ever portrayed the frustrations and small freedoms of women of the middle class of that era?

Thus the fact that a work was designed to be popular in its time and became so is not necessarily an indication, as some assume, that the writer was someone who earned that popularity by pandering to the fantasies of his or her audience. In fact, a work's appeal might very well have stemmed from people's perceptions that the author was recording life truthfully.

That writers of novels which happen to fall into the category of the mystery, or better yet, crime fiction—a classification so broad and diverse as to be nearly meaningless—are indeed concerned with telling the truth as they see it, and as uncompromisingly as possible, is apparent in the authors discussed in this book. Africa is a tremendous and enormously varied continent, but those who write about the corners of it they know are quite serious about their work. They wish to entertain, but not at the expense of getting things down right.

The interview with the South African James McClure provides numerous illustrations of this. McClure says that his writing "is concerned with real, or near real, life and consequences." He speaks about his desire to reach as wide an audience as possible, in order to convey "the *experience* of the country," and he is impatient with other South African writers who ignore what he attempts to capture, "the sheer complexity of the nuances of life in South Africa." His dislike of stereotyping and of using novels to advance *a* political viewpoint at the expense of rendering those nuances, that diversity, is an indication of the seriousness with which he takes his writing: a seriousness which includes portraying the humor and playfulness which exists in the midst of undeniable grimness. Robin Winks would say that McClure has succeeded quite well. "There is a more subtle look at relations between the races in South Africa in the books of James McClure (and especially in *The Gooseberry Fool*) than in many a learned piece on apartheid" (*Modus Operandi*, p. 61).

Earl Bargainnier discusses the African novels of John Canaday, art historian and critic, who wrote under the pseudonym of Matthew Head. Head admits in the foreword to *The Devil in the Bush* to some inaccuracies in his novel but it is possible to learn much about life in central Africa during the 1940s. Canaday served as a member of the U.S. Board of Economic Warfare to the Belgian Congo in 1943 and he drew upon his experiences there in writing *The Devil in the Bush*, *The Congo Venus*, and *The Cabinda Affair*.

Sharon Russell's essay on Elspeth Huxley's African novels demonstrates the complex relationship between Huxley's fiction and her view of Africa. Period, character, and setting all play important roles in Huxley's mysteries. Their African nature in her work is a result of her life in Africa as a child and as an adult.

African themes in West German crime fiction reflect a growing awareness of Africa in West Germany. Dieter Reigel discusses several West German writers who either set their novels in Africa or use African characters visiting West Germany. Generally, the authors studied by Reigel emphasize that they have prejudices but they attempt to give an unbiased picture of Africa.

Steven R. Carter concentrates on one work of detective fiction, *Petals of Blood* by Ngugi wa Thiong'o. Ngugi's harmonious blending of elements of African nature with elements of detective fiction enriches the form. He demonstrates that a creative master with insight can enlarge and modify any genre, no matter how rigid the format.

The works of Wessel Ebersohn, discussed by Fred Isaac, demonstrate how mystery fiction can be enlarged to include discussions of serious moral questions. Ebersohn's novels deal with the emotional quality that evil releases in people—all people, whether African or other.

John Wyllie wrote a series of mysteries set in Africa that explore both traditional and Western values. They have opened up for Western readers a continent seldom covered in detective fiction.

Mystery/crime authors must achieve a reasonable degree of accuracy in their settings if they are to maintain the credibility of their readers. The only alternative is to create a totally fictitious location. Even then, the reader may gain insights into the author and his society.

## 4 Mysteries of Africa

Fiction, in general, can provide "painless" lessons in history. The lessons must be evaluated carefully, but so too must the lessons provided by the "scholar." Mystery/crime fiction cannot replace scholarship and, indeed, is not intended to. It can, however, provide a valuable supplement as it entertains. With that caveat in mind, read on.

Don Wall
Eugene Schleh

# Chapter 1
# Colonial Mysteries

## Eugene Schleh

Authors who set their mysteries in Africa have a very wide range of experience with the continent and this is clearly shown in their work. Some seem to have stuck a pin in a map and thus come up with a setting. Francis Clifford's *The Green Fields of Eden* is set on an imaginary Spanish island off the African coast. After he describes three young women (passing "along the broken pavement's edge, baskets on their heads. . . . Africa was in their erect, loose-limbed walk; Spain in their chaste yet proud presentation of themselves.") the rest of the novel could as well be set in Madrid.

At the other end of the spectrum M.M. Kaye, Matthew Head, and Elspeth Huxley bring extensive experience and color to their work. Kaye followed her soldier husband to his varied assignments. She describes how she took extensive notes at each post and later used them in her geographically ranging novels. Matthew Head spent some time working in the Congo for the U.S. government and could provide extensive setting on the Congo and neighboring territories. Elspeth Huxley was born in London but raised in Kenya and later became a noted Africanist. The Africa portrayed by all three is definitely white colonial Africa with a bias toward settler territories like Kenya with its larger white population. This establishes the pattern for virtually all of the mysteries; they are part of the white culture and almost always involve Europeans. Detectives, victims, and criminals are almost all Europeans. The crimes often take place in the cities, themselves a European phenomenon, although they may appear rather strange to a newcomer. Head ranges along the west coast from Leopoldville,

5

# 6 Mysteries of Africa

Congo ("It was a pleasant little city, though, with two daily newspapers, one functioning movie, and three ice-cream and pastry parlors."), to Pointe Noire, French Congo ("a big, sprawled-out, fly-blown, ill-tempered town knocked flat on its back by the heat"), to Portuguese, Cabinda ("...a few modern brick or concrete structures which make the place more habitable even if less picturesque.") (E).* Other favorites seem to be Nairobi, Kenya, and perhaps least European, Zanzibar City. Whichever is the setting, however, it must be remembered that it is only the European sector of the city, no matter how many Africans may live in adjacent townships. These are simply acknowledged but remain unknown, such as Jack Iams description of Poto Poto and Bas Congo on the edges of Brazzaville, French Congo, ("which lay like teeming colonies of ants") (M).

Head demonstrates how casually Europeans can ignore the Africans when he describes Leopoldville, Congo as having "60,000 or 600,000 blacks, I've read both figures, but it doesn't make a difference. There are an awful lot of them, segregated in their own tremendous village..." (F). These Africans provide background whether they be farm laborers, low-ranked policemen, mine workers, porters, or the ubiquitous, innumerable servants. Iams has a visiting American impressed because his host has a servant while the host thinks: "I didn't tell him that there was also a cook, a washboy, and a *marmiton*—the boy's boy, or sort of a gentleman's gentleman's gentleman" (M). The record seems to be held by Head's Hooper Taliaferro who lives with three other Americans and together they regularly employ from a dozen to eighteen boys, the highest paid of whom was the cook at eight dollars a month (E). The Africans are usually dismissed as inefficient (E), slow (P), superstitious (B), witchcraft ridden (N), having no sense of time (H), or just having different thought processes (N). At best they can take care of African aspects of a situation such as using a black policeman to question other Africans (M); to let them question whites would be too insulting.

*Letter references are to books in the accompanying, alphabetized bibliography

Since most of the murders are committed with guns, this seems to rule out African suspects since the revolver is a "white man's weapon" (A), Africans "do not usually play with guns" (R), and the "average African gets no pleasure out of just shooting an enemy. He prefers to kill him slowly, and watch him suffer" (N). Africans are said to prefer poisoning, stabbing, and spearing (K).

Very late in the colonial period there appeared some "bridge novels" which began to prepare the reader for a new Africa. Political parties were developing, often with ethnic support (J) and an educated African couple could have on their wall a picture of Julius Nyerere, then leader of Her Majesty's opposition in the legislature and later President of Tanzania (D). Africans are portrayed as knowing changes are coming. While a European police officer investigates a murder in *The Merry Hippo*, his assistant, an African sergeant, patiently waits to take over his job. Huxley also presents what is possibly the most cautious yet prepared African character. He has one son in Moscow studying radio mechanics, a daughter in Chicago (industrial nutrition), another daughter in Allahabad (law), a younger son in Peking ("no one knew what he was studying") and another daughter "poised between animal husbandry in Dundee, electronics in Hanover and Slavonic cultures in Split" (J). By the 1960s it had even become acceptable to have an African as a major character, particularly political figures who are killed (O,Q). After a half century of Europeans, in and out of novels, doing their best to ignore Africans, Van Wyck Mason's hero Col. Hugh North admits: "I wish I knew more about Africa and Africans." (Q) The winds of change were blowing.

## Works Cited

A   Best, Herbert. *The Mystery of the Flaming Hut*. New York & London: Harper and Brothers Publishers, 1932.

B   Butler, K.R. *A Fall of Rock*. London: Geoffrey Bles, 1967.

C   Clifford, Frances. *The Green Fields of Eden*. Leicester: Ulverscroft, 1963.

D   Edqvist, Dagmar. *Black Sister*. London: Michael Joseph, 1963.

E   Head, Matthew. *The Cabinda Affair*. New York: Perennial Library (Harper & Row Publishers), 1981.

F____ *Congo Venus*. Harper & Row Publishers, 1982.

G——— *The Devil in the Bush.* New York: W.W. Norton & Company, Inc., 1945.

H    Huxley, Elspeth. *The African Poison Murders.* New York: Perennial Library (Harper & Row Publishers), 1981.

I    ——— *A Man From Nowhere.* London: Chatto & Windus, 1964.

J    ——— *The Merry Hippo.* London: Chatto & Windus, 1963.

K    ——— *Murder at Government House.* New York & London: Harper & Brothers Publishers, 1937.

L    ——— *Murder on Safari.* New York: Perennial Library (Harper & Row Publishers), 1982.

M    Iams, Jack. *The Body Missed the Boat.* New York: William Morrow and Company, 1947.

N    Kaye, M.M. *Death in Kenya.* New York: St. Martin's Press, 1983.

O    ——— *Death in Zanzibar.* New York: St. Martin's Press, 1983.

P    Lloyd, Lavander. *The Linton Memorial.* London: Longmans, Green and Co., 1957.

Q    Mason, Van Wyck. *Zanzibar Intrigue.* Garden City, N.Y.: Doubleday and Company, Inc., 1963.

R    Scholey, Jean. *The Dead Past.* New York: Garland Publishing Inc., 1983.

# Chapter 2
# Matthew Head's Dr. Mary Finney and Hooper Taliaferro Novels

**Earl F. Bargainnier**

Four of the six novels written in the decade from 1945 to 1955 by John Canaday, the art historian and critic for the New York *Times*, under the pseudonym of "Matthew Head," feature the cases of Dr. Mary Finney as narrated by Hooper Taliaferro.[1] He chose a pseudonym partially from fear of failure but also that he could "save my own name for writing about art. . . . I picked the name Matthew Head because I thought the combination of Matthew and Head looked faintly sinister."[2] Although he stated that he was dissatisfied with mysteries that "told little about the murderer and the murderee" and so decided to write his own, there is little more about those two figures in those four novels than in dozens of others. The setting, comedy and secondary characters contribute greatly to the entertaining liveliness of the novels, but the two major characters and the interplay between them are the principal elements of the works' success as novels of sophisticated detection.

Head is not a particularly innovative plotter. He follows essentially the same formula in each of his novels. Hooper has an experience involving murder, he relates to Dr. Finney what has happened—thrice while riding in a car, she then undertakes an investigation, and the murderer is discovered—again in three of the cases, the murderer confesses. Because of this formula, there is a disarrangement of time sequence, especially in *The Cabinda*

Published in *Clues*, vol. 4, no. 1 (Spring/Summer 1983). Reprinted with permission.

9

*Affair* and *The Congo Venus*, and this allows for effective misdirection through Hooper's misinterpretations or omissions in relating past events. (On the other hand, *The Devil in the Bush* is unnecessarily confusing as to the positions and relationships of the people—murderer, victims and suspects—at the Congo-Ruiz agricultural station.) The murderers are generally revealed early for they are rather obvious. In two cases they are "nicer" than their victims, whereas in the other two they are selfish egoists and the victims are sympathetic. Motives are passion or greed, and methods are not original. Head has to find other means of giving his novels their distinctiveness, for his plots would hardly have made them so, but fortunately he did.

The first three of the novels are set in Africa: *The Devil in the Bush* in Kivu province of the Belgian Congo, *The Congo Venus* in that colony's capital, Leopoldville, and *The Cabinda Affair* in the tiny Portuguese enclave of Cabinda at the mouth of the Congo River. *Murder at the Flea Club* is set in Paris, but could easily be in any European city. Although Head's Forward to the first novel admits that there are inaccuracies, "intentional and unimportant," a reader learns much of life in central Africa during the 1940s. Since the author served as a member of the U.S. Board of Economic Warfare mission to the Belgian Congo in 1943, he knew enough about life there to include such esoterica as the importance of the native servants' feet for prestige, the effect of guinea worms, banana beer "spiced with the carcasses of drowned flies" (*Devil*, 20), and the ingredients of palm-oil chop, the Congolese chicken stew. *The Congo Venus* details the insular life of Leopoldville, a little world of pretension, social-climbing, gossip and boredom, and all three African novels stress the precautions required to survive heat-stroke, amoebic dysentery and other perils of life in the tropics. The perils are not just physical; Dr. Finney gives Hooper a lecture on what Africa does to most white men, part of which is:

People change when they come out here. They go on acting the same to hide the change, but they make up a new character for themselves to keep laid over the change, but whatever you do you'll find more false faces per capita among the white men along the equator than you could find scare-faces if you searched every witch doctor's hut in the Congo. There's some kind of devil out here in the bush that changes people.(*Devil*, 40-41).

The everpresent sense of danger, other than murder, whether physical or mental, provides an additional layer of suspense, and the exoticism of African life creates an unusual background for the investigation of crime.

The crimes of the novels are blended with comedy of action and characterization, much of which, as will be seen, is the result of Hooper Taliaferro's personality, which is the narrative voice. Head's ability to seamlessly join comedy to detection is exceptional, for he never resorts to extraneous set-pieces. One of the best examples of this ability occurs in *The Congo Venus*. A Belgian lady's obsessive love for her Siamese cat, that cat's Garfield-like nature, and the lady's excruciating cello-playing in the Leopold String Quartet combine in one of the funniest musical recitals in fiction. The recital leads to what is called "the Great Stringed Instrument Schism" and more significantly to murder. As comic as the recital is, it is an integral element in the motive for murder and could not be omitted—though it is difficult to imagine any reader wishing away an episode so hilarious. Many secondary characters also contribute to the comic tone. Hooper's boss, Tommy Slattery, and his fellow-worker, Schmitty, are recurrent characters, who trade quips and sexual information and advice with him, particularly Slattery, who is always on the lookout for what he calls "hod-ziggadies." In *The Congo Venus* one meets the disreputable Dr. Gollmer and his two young mistresses, Lala and Baba, happily cavorting in a pool at night and eventually leaving for a snug life in a Marseilles brothel. Quite different is the young, handsome, intelligent, ultra-correct government agent Cotter, who makes Hooper feel inferior and resentful in *The Cabinda Affair*; since Hooper is the narrator, Cotter comes across as a satiric version of the priggish young-man-most-likely-to-succeed. The Parisian *Murder at the Flea Club* contains more such comic characters than the others. The denizens of that nightclub include the much-married Mrs. Jones, who could be a satire on Barbara Hutton; Bibi, an endearing dumb-blonde prostitute; and Freddie Fayerweather (born Frederick Gratzhaufer), a rich young American who has yet to decide whether he is gay or straight, but who has the manner of the former at its most extreme. Also present is Mrs. Jones' lawyer, succinctly described as "well born, well bred, well connected, well groomed, and stupid" (208). Such characters are both amusing and effective as witnesses and suspects, but they are very much subordinate to the two principals, as well as to another character related to them.

Dr. Mary Finney is fifty years old in the first novel. A native of Fort Scott, Kansas (the birthplace of her creator), she has spent nearly thirty years travelling around central Africa in her rickety station wagon with a Necessity Bag of instruments and medicine as a medical missionary, accompanied by Miss Emily Collins. She says that Emily works "the soul-and-hymn department" while she ministers to the flesh, and she is proud of her work. "I'm a perfectly honest missionary and I'm a damn good tropical doctor" (*Cabinda*, 166). Aside from a boy working in her father's feed store who attracted her when she was eighteen and one love affair in Africa, with the victim of *The Devil in the Bush*, her private life is unknown, which is the way she wants it: "I have stopped arguing with Emily over the relationship of the body and the soul, because I'm sick of the first, and the second is my own business" (*Devil*, 143). Her appearance is far from alluring, but it is impressive. Though not fat, she is "solid and hillocky," and her utter disdain for fashion emphasizes her bulkiness. She has coarse, carroty hair, big hands and a bright reddish face sprinkled "pleasantly" with large freckles. More important than physical appearance in creating her impressiveness is her manner. She is forthright and without pretense—and not fooled by it in others. She is given a medal by the Belgian government and is the guest of the Surete in Paris, but such official recognition means little to her. She swears occasionally; as a doctor, is unembarrassed by bodily functions, ordering Hooper on one of their jaunts to relieve himself in the bushes; and becomes furious at attempts to patronize her, as when Hooper says he will call her "Miss Mary": "That's the dirtiest, meanest, low-downest remark anybody ever made to me" (*Devil*, 78). She is a take-charge person: active, assertive, demanding, distrustful and often gruff. The gruffness, however, is mitigated by her basic kindness, which is evident in Hooper's repeated statements that "Somehow all the words she used sounded abrupt and rude, but she spoke with such an air of honest good humor that the effect was warm and friendly" (*Devil*, 48). This gruff kindness extends even to murderers; at the end of *Murder at the Flea Club*, she says, "Well, it's always fun until you catch them, then you're awfully let down. I hate to see even a son-of-a-bitch in such bad trouble" (261).

Nevertheless, this strong, honest and kind woman does catch murderers. Her practicality and common sense combine with her scientific training and her long experience of dealing with all sorts of people to form her methods of detection. It is her interest in people that motivates her: "What the hell, Hoop, I like watching people and figuring them out and trying to figure why they do what they do" (*Devil*, 76). Her evidence more often consists of words and actions of people than of physical objects. Though she is active in interviewing suspects and wants to be at the scene of the crime, she is a ratiocinative detective. As Hooper realizes, when she gets a deadpan expression on her face, she is concentrating all of her mind on what he has told her and what she has discovered. Her most detailed explanation of her method appear in *Murder at the Flea Club*:

Fingerprints and all that stuff I don't know anything about. But what I figure is, if you examine the lives of the people all around the victim you find some things in their lives that don't explain themselves. And in the victim's life too. Now if you can invent an explanation that fills all the holes, it might be the true one. You invent explanations no matter how unsupported they may seem to be except by one little inconsistency in that person's life, and if the same explanation explains away the inconsistencies in another's, then maybe you're getting things to dovetail. (36)

Such a method requires imagination, but even more a knowledge of people, a knowledge which she has gained in her years as a medical missionary. She is also persistent, even when as in *The Devil in the Bush* and *The Congo Venus* no one else sees any reason for an investigation, for when she "gets mixed up in something, she's mixed up in it for keeps, until the thing is settled" (*Cabinda*, 105). Like other fictional detectives, she refuses to tell what she knows, while being very demanding in that respect of others, especially Hooper: "I tell you I've got to get everything you can give me. I'll pick and choose the pieces that mean something. All you have to do is talk. The less you try to think, the better" (*Venus*, 41). The job of thinking is for her. Dr. Mary Finney is the missionary as detective, and she ranks among the most formidable of female amateur sleuths.

Her companion during her thirty years in Africa is Emily Collins. She is a caricature, at times a gross caricature, of the spinster missionary. Born in Milford, Connecticut, she speaks Swahili with a New England accent. Her origin is exemplified by her puritanism, which is explained as repressed sexuality. Dr. Finney says Emily has "a classic case of New England girlhood...I'd rather have syphilis" (*Devil*, 47). Her puritanism expresses itself in her continually pulling her skirts down, her innocence as when she meets a prostitute and unknowingly describes her as very "quiet and sweet," and shocked responses to Dr. Finney's openness about physical matters. On the other hand, she occasionally shows an inconsistently liberal attitude, especially in *The Congo Venus*, where after reading a copy of *Esquire*, she remarks, "After I figured out the first cartoon, the rest were easy. They all seem to be based on the same general idea" (121), and upon learning that Dr. Gollmer is going to live from the sexual earnings of his two young women, says "in a tone of innocent wisdom," "Well, why not, if it makes everybody happy?" (207). Nevertheless, this ninety-four pound, talcumed, middle-aged spinster, who looks like "a bunch of faggots tied up in a rag" (*Devil*, 121) or like Lillian Gish in *Birth of a Nation*, is supposedly a mass of repressions, evidenced to Hooper by her silk robe with gigantic red poppies, her stated sense of a lack of completeness, and her rare but violent tantrums toward Dr. Finney.

Since she represents the spirit, or the soul-and-hymn department, in her collaboration with Dr. Finney, one would expect her to play a large role in the cases, and she does not. Dr. Finney orders her to spread rumors in *The Congo Venus* and to shoot a man in *The Cabinda Affair*. She complies, but faints immediately after the shooting, while later considering it exciting to Dr. Finney's distress. Emily is ever willing to help, but her analyses of cases are always wrong. But underneath her unattractive, meek exterior, she has a powerful will; as one character put it: "Don't underestimate Emily Collins...She may look like a mouse but she's got the determination of a mad water buffalo" (*Devil*, 59), and Hooper thinks she has a lot of "spunk." She has to have that quality to have survived the rigors of Africa from approximately 1925 to 1955. Though she is not always consistent as a character, she provides a contrasting companion for Dr. Finney, one who emphasizes the latter's practicality, lack of reticence and dominant personality, without detracting from the plot of the two central characters, and that is Head's major reason for including her.

Another reason is that she provides Dr. Finney with someone to whom she can compare Hooper's innocence; she even calls him "Emily dear." She says that he is a nice boy, as Emily is "a real nice girl just turning forty-nine" (*Cabinda*, 144) and that if he wore skirts, he would "be pulling at them all the time" (*Devil*, 78). In fact, her treatment of Hooper can only be called condescending, in spite of her fondness for him. She pats him on the knee when she is pleased with his performance, continually uses "nice boy" or "little boy" in addressing him, refers to herself as his "Aunt Mary," and in spite of her own lapses upbraids him for swearing, which she considers unbecoming in a young man. Her attitude may be seen in the following exchange:

> "You, Hoop—you're sort of a trusting, think-the-best-of-people, innocent-type boy."
> "Well, thanks."
> "I hadn't thought of it as a compliment." (*Flea*, 34)

She also withholds information from him and plays investigatory tricks, but is angry when, from delicacy, he does not tell her everything in *Murder at the Flea Club*: "I respect your motives as a gentleman, but I deplore the hell out of your attitude as my co-sleuth" (150).

Of course he is not really her co-sleuth; he is her supplier of information and her Watson, the recounter of her cases. In those capacities, however, his personality—not hers—dominates the novels. Whether or not his creator modeled him upon himself, there are autobiographical features. Though some eight to ten years younger, Hooper is almost as interested in art as John Canaday is; he collects African sculpture in the first three novels and in the last has opened an art gallery in Paris. Canaday served the American government in the Congo in 1943 and then in the Marines until the end of the war, the first novel being written while he was in the South Pacific. Hooper serves in an identical position in the Congo, then enters the Marines, but returns to the Congo after the war on another government mission. He comes from an academic background, like Canaday, but his field is not art, but botany. He is "a tropical products man," the reason for his academic leave from an unnamed university to fulfill his government work. Though never stated, Hooper is obviously a southerner since his name is pronounced "Tolliver"—Canaday taught at the University of Virginia from 1938 to 1950.[3] Called Hoop or Hoopie by friends, he is in his late twenties and early thirties in the novels. Dr. Finney's remarks indicate that his looks are not exceptional, and the only comment he makes about the matter occurs in *Murder at the Flea Club*: "No detailed description of me is necessary. Medium as to looks, intelligence, ambition, and so on, but I get along. My only real talent is as a spectator. I am one of the best people to be found anywhere, when it comes to just watching. It is really my life work" (2).

His delight in watching others makes him a good narrator, but other qualities are equally important in his personality; he is bright, normal, affable, romantic, sympathetic to those in trouble, easy-going (one character says that "sometimes I think you're almost too broad-minded" [*Flea*, 78]), sometimes homesick, desirous of friends, and very open. Like most young men, he has sex very much on his mind. In *The Devil in the Bush*, he states, "The first thing I always wonder about new people is what they manage to do for a living and how they arrange their sex life, because it seems to be that those two activities plus sleep and a movie or two account for most people's twenty-four hours a day" (25). One of his functions in the novels is to provide a sexual, if not romantic, interest. In the first he engages in sex, in the next two he almost does, and in the last an attempt is made to seduce him, though not for reasons of passion. All four novels show that whatever his desires, he has scruples. He seduces a quite willing young Belgian girl in *The Devil in the Bush,* but—in spite of Dr. Finney's importuning— refuses to marry her, for he knows that neither of them would be happy, yet his conscience bothers him. Circumstances prevent any sexual activity in *The Cabinda Affair* and *The Congo Venus,* though there are women he desires in both, and the sense is that he feels it is just as well, for both women are married. He also disapproves of those white men who have sexual relations with native women, not for racial reasons, but because "that's low stuff and unsatisfying, without the eating and drinking and dancing and companionship that make the rest of it worth while" (*Devil,* 26). One can only call him a romantic in these novels, but in *Murder at the Flea Club* Head seems to have attempted touches of the hard-boiled detective as regards women. On meeting a fashionable society woman, he inspects her and then concentrates on her shoes:

shoes composed of a high heel, an invisible sole, and about five straps per shoe—at, conservatively, somewhere around twenty dollars a strap. They had been designed on the premise that the wearer would never encounter any hazard of weather greater than one step from a taxi to a marqueed entrance, and that they would make any man aware of his own burliness. They did me. I felt taller and hairier. (9)

However, a later attempted seduction of him by the same woman makes him as "suspicious as hell" and leads him to the observation: "If this is a make, I thought, it's going to have to be awfully quiet and elegant. It would be a shame if anybody got rowdy" (102). The humor of the statements undercuts the machoism. All in all, Hooper has a healthy attitude about sex, and Head's treatment of his sexual nature is refreshing, considering the period in which the novels were written.

The reason Hooper is inadequate as a detective is that he is swayed by emotion:

Miss Finney told me that the process that went on inside my head when I thought I was thinking was nothing more than an exercise in the distortion of obvious fact by the application of sentimental prejudice. And it is certainly true that it is difficult for me to believe that anybody I like is really capable of evil or that anybody I dislike isn't full of it. (*Cabinda*, 177)

Added to this indictment is her statement that "You've got the openest goddam pan I ever saw on a boy in my life" (*Venus*, 8). He is aware that he allows his feelings for others to influence his judgement, calling himself "a damn fool" and "a chump," and admitting, "There was hardly a person at the Congo-Ruiz who wasn't trying to fool me one way or another, and most of them got away with it" (*Devil*, 33). His problem is that he accepts the obvious—Dr. Finney never does—or admires good looks or welcomes friendship too quickly. His easy-going nature causes him to like anyone who is pleasant to him, and since his likes are immediate, he is often blinded to the true character of those he encounters. Hooper is not stupid, just a man of feeling; when he has no emotional ties to a person, he can see that person as he or she is. For example, he can recognize an actress-wife's hysterics over her husband's disappearance for what they are: "The script was terrible, like anything an actress writes for herself to play" (*Devil*, 119). But such perceptiveness about people is rare, and so he has to wait, with the reader, for Dr. Finney to reveal whodunit and why.

In spite of his fallibility as a detective, Hooper is an excellent reporter of facts. He claims in *The Cabinda Affair* that he has trained himself in remembering details:

I used to practice by listening to people on the street and then sitting down and writing out as near as I could just what they had said, or having someone read to me out of a book, dialogue, and setting that down, although that wasn't as good an exercise, since the way you remember is by the spontaneous inflections and contrasts in voices, and the gestures. But I had got pretty good at it. (186)

Such a statement can be dismissed as an author's ploy to explain his narrator's ability to remember verbatim conversations, as well as past details of all sorts, which it probably is. However, no explanation or apology is required from Head for Hooper's style as a narrator. His colloquial narration of the novels is natural and possesses, as an early reviewer noted, "limpid ease."

If the cliché that the style is the man has any validity, then Hooper Taliaferro is a superb example. His style as narrator is inseparable from his personality as a character. The only specific aspect of that style which demands mention is his use of figures of speech. Academics are fond of them, and Head gives Hooper a generous number. A few are unnecessarily "arty," such as "The exquisite furniture sat within the pastel glow with the air of aristocrats awaiting the call to the tumbrils" (*Flea*, 6), but most are strikingly apt in their comic hyperbole. African banana beer smells "like a cross between chocolate and paint remover" (*Devil*, 20). During a fast car ride, Emily bounces around "like a dried pea in a cement mixer" (*Devil*, 99). In a small African town Hooper shaves "in a mirror that made you look like something that was just coming to the surface after three or four weeks," and the same town's hotel kitchen has "the fine sanitary quality of a badly run-down leprosarium" (*Cabinda*, 45, 48). Hooper's figures of speech, like his openness, his colloquialness, and his altogether human weaknesses as a detective, make him an engaging narrator: the perfect Watson for the practical, no-nonsense, formidable Dr. Finney.

These four novels from 1945 to 1955 (three in print in 1982) are examples of the American form of the sophisticated, comic, "classical" detective novel. Less complex in plot than many others, the novels more than compensate for this lack—if that is what it is—by the exotic settings, the wit, the style and the two central characters. They are generally referred to as the Dr. Mary Finney novels, but because of the narrator's personality totally controlling the tone and pace, they deserve to be known as the Dr. Mary Finney and *Hooper Taliaferro* novels.

# Notes

[1]The editions of the four novels by Matthew Head considered in this essay are listed below, preceded by the original date of publication and followed by an abbreviation to be used where necessary for citation within the text:

1945   *The Devil in the Bush* (New York: Avon, n.d.). (*Devil*)
1949   *The Cabinda Affair* (New York: Harper & Row, 1981). (*Cabinda*)
1950   *The Congo Venus* (New York & London: Garland, 1976). (*Venus*)

1955   *Murder at the Flea Club* (New York: Harper & Row, 1981) (*Flea*)

Other mystery novels by Head are *The Smell of Money* (1943), *The Accomplice* (1947) and *Another Man's Life* (1953).

[2]Quoted in *Contemporary Authors*, Vol. 13-16, p. 135.

[3]Jacques Barzun and Wendell Hertig Taylor seem puzzled by Hooper's last name (*A Catalogue of Crime* [New York: Harper & Row, 1971], p. 231). Most southerners would know that Taliaferro is pronounced "Tolliver" more often than it is "Telfair" or as the spelling would indicate. Canaday's teaching in the South for nearly fourteen years is the reason for this pronunciation. Only in the edition I have of *The Congo Venus* is Hooper's last name spelled Tolliver, and that edition is one of the "Fifty Classics of Crime Fiction: 1900-1950," edited by Barzun and Taylor. Did they change the spelling?

# Chapter 3
## Elspeth Huxley's Africa:
## Mystery and Memory

### Sharon A. Russell

For most readers Elspeth Huxley is best known as the author of *The Flame Trees of Thika* (1959), an autobiographical work that was the source of a popular Public Television series. But Huxley, who was born in 1907, spent her formative years in Kenya and returned to Africa several times in her later life.

Her experiences in Kenya form the basis for much of her writing. In addition to travel books, autobiographies, and biographies she also has written several novels with African settings. Five of these fictional works are generally considered mysteries: *Murder at Government House* (1937), *Murder on a Safari* (1938), *The African Poison Murders* (1939), *The Incident at the Merry Hippo* (1964), and *A Man from Nowhere* (1965). A sixth, *The Red Rock Wilderness* (1957),[1] has not usually been considered part of her work in the mystery genre even though it relates directly to these other novels. All six are closely connected to Huxley's African experiences, five have an African setting and, in the other, the African landscape constantly intrudes on the English setting. But the relationship between Huxley's fiction and her view of Africa is extremely complex. An analysis of these novels within the context of Huxley's autobiographical non-fiction helps in an understanding of the role of Africa in her genre fiction and the extent to which her experiences have influenced it.

21

## 22 Mysteries of Africa

While Huxley started writing mysteries in 1937 it was not until 1959 that she published the first in a series of autobiographical works, *The Flame Trees of Thika*. It was followed by *On the Edge of the Rift* (1962), *Love Among the Daughters* (1968) and, most recently, *Out in the Midday Sun* (1985). The distance between the first and last of these works can be measured by her changing attitude towards head wear. The opening of *The Flame Trees of Thika* contains a description of Elspeth's carefully covered head as she and her mother travel to Thika. In the first three books real names are covered as carefully as the character's heads. In *Out in the Midday Sun* the first chapter is titled "Hat Overboard" and contains a description of Elspeth's loss of her hat; she remains bare-headed for the rest of her time in Africa. And, in this volume, for the first time, she reveals the real names of the people she discusses.

There are three common elements in Huxley's autobiographies and mysteries. Period, character, and setting are basic in literature, but their uniquely African nature in her work is a product of her experiences as both child and adult on that continent. It is the land, Africa itself, that is primary in both fact and fiction. Elspeth's parents came to Africa in search of a new challenge. They were drawn to the openness of the African landscape at the same time that they attempted to cultivate it through various experiments with farming. It is ironic that for them to be successful they needed aspects of the civilization they attempted to leave behind. Crops must get to market; roads and railways have to be built. All of the early colonists brought with them the seeds of their own destruction. In both her autobiographical works and her fiction Huxley's description of the land and its function as a setting reflects this ambiguity in the early settlers' lives. Africa is both a land to be developed, a home for those farmers who attempt to re-create the farms of their past in this new territory, and a wilderness for the hunters who started out by emulating the natives they found on the land but who brought in new technology ultimately destroying the very sport they created.

Inherent in her presentation of the changing relationship between the land and its various inhabitants is Huxley's constant sense of the passage of time. While the radical alterations in the

African landscape and socio-economic structure would be apparent to anyone who had spent some time on the continent, in Huxley's work these changes become more significant because they are tied to her own maturation process. In her work there are four distinct periods in the development of modern Africa, specifically Kenya. The period before World War I, covered in *The Flame Trees of Thika*, is a time of innocence for both Elspeth and Kenya. She grows up with the country., It is an era that she returns to in her biography of Lord Delamere, the early governor of Kenya (*White Man's Country*), but it is not represented in her mysteries.

The second period in Huxley's work is easily defined as the time between the wars. At this point, Africa has really been "discovered" by both tourist and immigrant; it is the era of the safari. Elspeth and her mother return to the Africa they left at the end of *The Flame Trees of Thika*. But her parents find the old coffee farm too close to civilization, and they move to the area described in *On the Edge of the Rift*. Elspeth must finally leave Africa during this period for the college activities described in *Love Among the Daughters*. She also recalls this era in *Out in the Midday Sun*, the book where, from the perspective of the present, she is most aware of the changes in the world of the thirties. Her three most traditional mysteries were also written toward the end of this period.

The era immediately after World War II is much less clearly defined. It is the point of transition between the height of Great Britain's involvement with the African Colonies and their independence, the period of the painful change from colonialism to nationalism. At this point Huxley is only a visitor to Africa, although she retains her active involvement through membership in the Monckton Commission which dealt with the British government's interest in uniting Rhodesia and Nyasaland. Huxley writes many books about her travels in Africa during these almost twenty years. (Kenya's independence was achieved on December 12, 1963, Uganda, October 9, 1962, and Tanganyika, December 9, 1961— author's note *With Forks and Hopes*.) While this is a particularly fruitful period for Huxley's non-fiction and is the source of later mysteries, only *The Red Rock Wilderness* was published at this time.

The post-colonial period is current history. While Huxley has written extensively about the immediate transition period, it is only quite recently that she returns to the locations and people of her youth. *Out in the Midday Sun* is a kind of summing up of her personal thoughts about Kenya. The two mysteries, *The Incident at the Merry Hippo* and *A Man from Nowhere* deal with the very recent past. As she says, "People say that it is a mistake to go back, but I think this is so only if you expect things to be much the same or, if they changed, to have changed for the worst." (*Out*, p. 224) Unlike many of the colonists that she describes, Huxley is able to accept the changes that have occurred.

The third element connecting Huxley's fiction and non-fiction is her view of the people of Kenya. These people can be further divided into three distinct factions: the Africans, those tribes who lived in Kenya before the white man and who now, once more, control the country; the colonists, a collection of people, most from Great Britain, who came to make some kind of fortune in this new world; and, finally, a variety of visitors, from members of the foreign office to tourists on safaris. As with the other elements, Huxley always avoids simplification and obvious stereotypes. Her autobiographical works are filled with examples of strong individuals struggling to survive, but she does not ignore the complexity of the society around her. The colonials included fortune hunters as well as farmers. In the early days, the white colony was small and, especially in Nairobi, marital relationships were not always stable; Huxley's characters reflect the complex structure of this society. The diversity and dignity of the Africans is always acknowledged by Huxley who was, no doubt, influenced by her parents' attitudes. In her later writing she has a fair evaluation of the Mau Maus and of Jomo Kenyatta and his development as a leader. (*Out*, pp. 201-203) The transients, too, are carefully examined. Huxley explains the difference between the training received in the diplomatic and colonial branches of the government (*Out*, p. 69) And her autobiographical works contain sharp observations of the various tourists and other non-settlers she encounters.

The connections between Huxley's autobiographies and mysteries go beyond the mere clichés of life influencing art. Since her autobiographical works were written beside her mysteries the elements of the former function in unique ways in the later. While it might seem that Huxley's Africa is a mere window dressing for her mysteries, adding a touch of glamour to the more traditional works and providing an exciting background for the thrillers, the elements of Huxley's autobiographies are transformed into the essentials of her fiction. This influence goes beyond the interesting but obvious use of African setting and plot elements to the formation of style and theme in these works. A close examination of the interrelationships of all of these elements in her mysteries reveals the essential nature of her African experiences for all of her writing.

The primary function of the elements of land, people and period is, of course, to create the atmosphere for Huxley's mysteries. Both *Murder at Government House* and *The Incident at the Merry Hippo* make similar uses of government settings. However character and location are treated much more gently in the earlier novel. The passage of time alters Huxley's view of British officials in Africa. In both novels the intended victim is the highest ranking official, a representative of the foreign office, rather than the Colonial government towards which Huxley displays the same attitude as that indicated in her other writings, officials in the latter lack the understanding of the local situation found in the former. While the murders in both books seem to be motivated by politics, they are actually the result of incidents from the past that are brought to the surface by recent events or by confrontations with people not seen for many years. This view of one's life as a continuum where the past is essential to an understanding of the present is certainly evident in all of Huxley's work.

But the changes that Huxley observes in Africa are revealed all the more strongly because of the similarity between the two works. *Murder at the Government House* is a locked room puzzle that is solved by the detective that she uses in her early mysteries, the head of the C.I.D. and a Canadian immigrant, Vachell. His character is probably modeled after Canadians Huxley described in *Love Among the Daughters*, men she met during her period of study at Cornell. In *The Incident at the Merry Hippo* official and amateur detective join forces, not unlike the assistance Vachell is given by the observant anthropologist, Miss Olivia Brandeis, but this time, the amateur is more successful, another in a series of indications that the British official hold is weakening in Africa. As in all of her writing, the characters in these books are balanced individuals, and even the murderers have both good and bad traits. Both books contain strong female figures similar to those encountered in Huxley's non-fiction. Although, in the later book, even the women are not free of the satire that colors the entire novel. It is as though humor is the only method that Huxley can find to deal with these incidents in a novel placed between two violent explorations of the land and its people, *The Red Rock Wilderness* and *A Man From Nowhere*.

The two mysteries that follow *Murder at the Government House*, *Murder on Safari* and *The African Poison Murders*, provide her most detailed exploration of the classic views of Africa: the safari and the farm. Both are traditional mysteries and continue to use Vachell as the detective. *Murder on Safari* acknowledges the changes that have already taken place in Africa; even in the thirties safaris are expensive and luxurious. As Danny de Mare, the head of the safari says,

Simba Ltd. has changed a lot since first I knew it. They started life by taking foot safaris from the coast to the Great Lakes before the days of railways. It took six months for the round trip. There were three or four hundred porters, sometimes each one with his sixty-pound load and a pair of boots slung around his neck. They had to carry beads and cloth to trade for food with the up-country natives. Now, of course, everything's done in lorries, even planes sometimes, with all home comforts laid on. Simba Ltd. do everything from the moment you get to Chania with your cheque-book to the moment you leave with your trophies. (p.17)

De Mare bears a striking resemblance to Baron Bror von Blixen-Finecke, famous for being a hunter as well as being the husband of Karen Blixen, and Chris Davis, the woman flyer who serves as scout for animals as well as his love interest on the safari, strongly resembles Beryl Markham who served a similar function for Blixen. Not only does Huxley know the kind of people who would organize and lead a safari but all of the details of a safari are also second nature to her. De Mare asks Vachell to join the safari in the guise of a hunter so that Vachell can investigate a robbery that has taken place, and he easily explains the rifles Vachell will need and the specific function of each. When the two men arrive at the camp site, the setting is described in such detail that it is easy to picture the entire scene.

Huxley's complex handling of her characters allows even the members of the safari to be portrayed sympathetically. The members of the safari are destroying the balance of nature without even paying the price of discomfort. But even though the characters require a certain level of comfort and want to take home appropriate trophies, they are not totally unconscious of what they are doing. One of the members has already made the transition from gun to camera, although he is implicated in arming natives just to get rare film footage. The love of hunting is off-set by an awareness of the loss of animals. Huxley's growing concern for animals becomes much more evident in *The African Poison Murders* where an insane person cruelly mutilates and destroys both domestic and wild animals. In this novel the future is foreshadowed clearly in the British title, *Death of an Aryan*. The sub-plot deals with the Nazi neighbor of the central characters, Karl Munson. Vachell is originally called in to investigate possible attacks that the Wests and other neighbors have received from Munson who is involved with the Bund. Munson and his wife are among the few totally unsympathetic characters Huxley creates. The other characters are like those interesting and eccentric people Huxley encountered in her youth. The Wests are attempting to start a dairy herd. Jolyot Anstey, a neighbor, who also farms, has his beans destroyed by the Munsons' wandering cattle. In addition to the mystery, other events in the novel constantly emphasize the fragility of life on these farms. Dennis West is killed by the murderer during a fire that threatens the farms. And, of course, all of the action takes place in country that is beautiful even if dangerous. "Beyond lay a view that, Vachell reflected, people might travel across half the world to see if it wasn't a British colony, and therefore taken for granted at home and unknown abroad." (p. 16) In this novel the beauty of the place is threatened, but peace is restored. War is still in the future, and it will not be fought by most of these people in this part of Africa.

Both *The Red Rock of Wilderness* and *A Man from Nowhere* present a view of a changed world. It is as though Huxley is attempting to find ways to deal with the problems that she sees in the land she loves. Both novels use a distancing device to handle these feelings. In *The Incident at the Merry Hippo* she resorts to satire and humor, but in the novels written before and after that book the themes are too serious for that kind of treatment. *The Red Rock of Wilderness* purports to be the journal of Andrew Colquhoun. As his father explains in the introduction, Andrew has retreated to Canada and left these journals with him. They are being published as a means of explaining the events that took place at Luala. The journals describe a quest that Andrew takes to meet Dr. Ewart Clausen and write his biography. This quest takes the young man into "the heart of darkness," Bamili rock, where much about Africa is revealed. In this novel, where Huxley uses real names for many places, an unusual practice for her, there is little hope expressed for the future of the continent. M. Riviere, the former district officer in French Equatorial Africa who has sent the journal to Andrew's father is fighting a holding operation as opposing forces struggle for control. Good people are caught between tribal leaders and large corporations, and no one is left untouched by the conflict.

In *The Man from Nowhere* Africa appears only in the flashbacks of the central character, Dick Heron. He comes from an unidentified country, but it is obvious the incidents he recalls are the Mau Mau attacks that occurred in Kenya in the fifties. His view of England is clearly that of Huxley, both find the country very small when compared with Africa. "To begin with, everything was tiny, almost miniature." (*Love*, p. 9) "...but Dick was amazed by the scale to which he couldn't grow accustomed—the smallness of everything." (p. 127) While in *The Red Rock Wilderness* the hero is horrified to find out that most of the characters have been destroyed or perverted by the environment, a view that results in a message that even the good-intentioned white man cannot withstand the confrontation with the primitive strength of the native, Dick Heron learns that the evil that he comes to avenge, the deaths of his brother and wife, directly and indirectly related to the Mau Maus, (his wife has committed suicide) cannot be simply resolved through the application of an eye for an eye. The complex situations that Dick Heron must deal with are beyond this simple farmer, and he, too, is ultimately destroyed by his African experiences.

Before he came, he'd taken the clear-cut, irreversible decision to exact a kind of wild justice—he knew the quotation. All doubts had been settled and buried. Like all wild things, this wild justice was true and honest a nature, uncorrupted by men. It was a part of the natural law—life for life, tooth for tooth, balance and order which were sweet things, harmony and reciprocity. (pp. 67-68)

But African justice can no longer work. Life has become too complex. Too much has changed; the simple resolutions of the early novels are no longer possible.

Huxley's contemplation of the changes in Africa and their reflection in these mysteries suggests that the African elements work on very deep levels in her works. They form the basis of style and theme in her mysteries. Huxley's metaphoric language always returns to her vision of Africa. In *Murder at Government House*, "Jeudwine lifted his hunched shoulders and withdrew his face from the safe like a lizard pulling back its scaly head after darting at a fly." (p. 45) A face is described: "Expressions raced across it as quickly as cloud shadows over the open plain on a windy day." (p. 100) But even in this early novel metaphor becomes the basis of action. Olivia Brandeis, the anthropologist, discovers that the African secret society that is thought to have some connection with the murder is composed of a group of Africans who mimic the English dinner party in an attempt to become as strong as the English. While this episode is ultimately a red herring, the actual solution is foreshadowed in the words of a witch doctor. It takes the Europeans a little longer to figure out his meaning and the solution.

The role of the native is not as significant in *Murder on a Safari*. While this novel continues the use of African metaphor, the plot is constructed around the actions of the safari, also a uniquely African event. When Vachell is asked to join the safari he responds, "It appeals like a swim in a pool full of crocodiles." (p. 6) And later a storm appears; "...the storm swooped down like a giant angry hawk with a scream of wind to herald its approach." (p. 159) In this novel the solution also grows out of an understanding of Africa. While the identification of guns and bullet is standard in detective fact and fiction, the type of bullet that would be used to shoot a specific kind of animal is information of primary importance for a safari. Just as the safari is integral to *Murder on Safari* so is the African farm and its unique situation essential to *The African Poison Murders*.

While this novel continues the use of African metaphor, it also further develops another aspect of Huxley's integration of Africa into her work: the description of nature which either directly precedes or follows a scene of violence. Even in *Murder at Government House*, which largely takes place indoors, the chapter which contains the murder opens with a description of the ground. In *The African Poison Murders* Vachell begins to doubt that there can be a reconciliation of these elements.

> The first thing Vachell saw in the morning was a fly-catcher with a white-rimmed eye sitting perkily on the window-sill, and beyond that a deep red rose swaying in a light breeze...Blood-lust and roses, the obscenity of madness and a purple waxbill swaying on a twig—such discordant elements could not be made to blend. But Bullseye's bandaged head, the revolver on a table, bloodstains over Vachell's dressing-gown, furnished proof that it was not a nightmare, and quelled, in doing so, a little of the brilliance of the sun. (p. 137)

As the title of this book suggests, the murder weapon is uniquely African. But the motive for the murders is not as closely tied to Africa as in the two earlier novels.

While *The Red Rock Wilderness* contains the same use of metaphor and the same alternation of violence and scenes from nature as can be found in the earlier books, the human violence is even more overwhelming, and it becomes impossible to maintain these distinctions. The African continent seems to create violence now that conflicts between black and white, civilization and nature escalate. In this novel the natives no longer have to imitate the white man to gain power. Native rituals are now understood to be powerful enough to conquer and control the interloper. And, for the first time, colonials are openly seen as interlopers, even from the point of view of the narrator, a European.

> And, after all, we're interlopers in this immense desert and plain with its bush-dotted gullies, its trodden cattle paths, its arid harshness, the bitter struggle for existence waged by every thorn bush, every water-storing bulb, every food-questing bird and preyed-on insect. We couldn't live here as these lean brown tribesmen do, following the herd, surviving on a few handfuls of millet and a cupful of rancid whey...
>
> We're interlopers and our stay may be a short one, but we shall be survived by our ideas, which already have cracked the mould of Africa and let in new forces, new patterns, to mingle with the old. (p. 60)

The conclusion of the novel continues to explore the irreconcilable differences that are threatening Africa in the fifties. While the reader knows what happened at Bamili rock, an official version of the truth is not possible. And even the central characters are too confused and exhausted to explain the events. New patterns still must fight old beliefs, and the corporations that are part of the new also bring their own corruption.

The struggle of opposing forces is treated satirically in *The Incident at the Merry Hippo*. As Dr. Burton observes, "Our only lasting achievement in Africa has been to destroy its mystery." (p. 52) Either because the imaginary locale is not eastern Africa, or because of the deliberately distancing tone, this mystery is the least directly connected to Africa in style and theme. While the African metaphor is still present, the implications are made explicit, and the mystery is not directly tied to Africa. Both motives and events could take place elsewhere. The most serious exploration of image occurs when Alex Burton and Thomasina Labouchere, personal assistant for the Connor Commission, meet at the Pig and Whistle in the mining camp. The veranda grill was built around a small pond inhabited by noisy frogs. Thomasina explains that the frogs have gotten too abundant so a baby crocodile has been placed in the pond. As she says, "It's only about a foot long, but it's growing rapidly and eating up the frogs. Every night the frog chorus diminishes a little. It's awfully sinister." (p. 132) This revelation forces Alex to reconsider his view of the pond. The menace beneath the surface becomes symbolic of both life in Hapana and the operation of the commission (p. 133). This image is so important to Huxley in this book that she returns to it near the end of the novel. Even in this mystery, with its lighter tone, there is an intensification of the images.

> Outside, in the morning sunlight, everything looked normal and serene. And yet there were spiders tearing live flies to bits, ants devouring grubs, buzzards pouncing on voles; the cycle of pain, destruction and rebuilding went on endlessly. She thought of the pond with its ferocious little crocodile, and every night the frog chorus growing weaker. Yet the pond looked calm and beautiful, the frogs croaked happily until a single snap silenced them forever. (p. 188)

Yet in this novel Huxley does provide a conventional resolution to the mystery. The murderer is revealed; the crime solved; the love relationship resolved. Even the Connor Commission continues with its work.

In *A Man from Nowhere* Huxley's unidentified African country once more seems to be Kenya, especially since the threat this time comes from Mau Mau-like forces. The conflict between African and English values is intensified by the use of the English setting. Africa appears only in flashbacks, flashbacks that become more and more painful for the reader and for Dick Heron as he re-experiences those events that have sent him to England for revenge. In this novel Huxley achieves an absolute unification of theme and those African elements present in her other works. The physical differences between England and Africa explored in the novel are externalizations of Dick Heron's growing internal conflict. The more that he becomes tamed by the English countryside and the English people that he meets the less is he able to carry out his single-minded quest for revenge whose source is in the Africa he has left. As in *The Red Rock Wilderness*, there is no easy solution to this conflict. *A Man from Nowhere* goes even further in its refusal to find a resolution for the problems it explores. In the earlier novel the hero is disillusioned, but he and his newly found love interest survive. In the later novel even love becomes a destructive factor for the central character, adding to the complexity of the decisions that he must make. Dick Heron clearly explains the position of the white settler in Africa and how it is different from that of the British gentleman farmer.

> It's all rather hard to explain. Here in England nothing ever really belongs to you, it's more as if you were sort of trustee... You can bring in a few changes but fundamentally you don't alter anything. And you hand it on very much as it was. (p. 290)

He contrasts this with what he did in Africa, clearing the land, building a home, and bringing new animals and plants to the farm. But the government, represented by his enemy in England, has forced the colonists to give back the land. He insists that in five years the land will be reclaimed by the wilderness, and there will be nothing left of his efforts. Neither Dick nor his wife is able to accept this change, and both are destroyed by it. In the bleakest ending of all of Huxley's mysteries there is no resolution. No one understands Dick's motives completely. The mystery that he brings from Africa dies with him.

The changing situation in Africa is reflected in Huxley's work as she moves from the classic mysteries of the thirties to the thrillers of the fifties and sixties. There is also an increase in violence in these novels. An innocent man is killed instead of the victim in *The Incident at the Merry Hippo*. In both *The Red Rock Wilderness* and *A Man from Nowhere* guilt and innocence become relative concepts even though in both novels an innocent and naive person is killed. The changing style of these novels reflects her understanding of the increasing complexity of the African situation. Just as the simplicity of *The Flame Trees of Thika* with its idyllic view of an African childhood where real characters are given fictional names gives way to the harsher realities of *Out in the Midday Sun* where actual photographs document past and present, so do the novels reflect these changes. The simple contrast between nature and man, the beauty and harmony of the natural world, are laid bare in the later books, revealing the harsh world that always existed below the surface. It is only after Huxley leaves the Africa of her childhood, the Africa presented in her early mysteries, that she recognizes the conflicts that must exist between colonist and native, between government and the governed where there can be no easy resolutions of these conflicts and where clear oppositions must give way to shades and shadows. In her later books Huxley acknowledges her past at the same time that she recognizes the problems that it has caused in the present. Finally, in *Out in the Midday Sun* she is able to deal with those changes and clearly express both sides of the problem. Unlike some of the settlers she encounters, she is able to understand and support her mother's position. Her mother sold the family farm at a loss to those Africans who had lived on it and worked for her, because otherwise they would have no place to go. In 1965 when she was eight Nellie Grant moved on to start a new life on a small farm in Portugal. (p. 233) Huxley ends this book with a visit to Kenya in 1983 for the celebration of twenty years of independence. The last chapter is also filled with a awareness of contrasts. She visits Major Esther Wambui Njombo, the daughter of their headman at the farm at Njoro. Huxley reflects on the changes in Nairobi and on the farm. But all of these reflections are now positive. Unlike the characters in her later mysteries, Huxley does survive, retaining the best of both England and Africa.

# Note

[1]The editions of Huxley's novels cited in the text are listed below; all references are indicated in the text and shortened titles are used when necessary for clarity. Novels: *Murder at Government House* (New York: Harper, 1937), *Murder on Safari* (New York: Harper and Row, 1982), *The African Poison Murders* (New York: Harper, 1939), *The Red Rock Wilderness* (New York: William Morrow, 1957), *The Incident at the Merry Hippo* (New York: William Morrow, 1964), *A Man from Nowhere* (New York: William Morrow, 1965). The British title of *The African Poison Murders* is *Death of an Aryan*; the British title of *The Incident at the Merry Hippo* is *The Merry Hippo*. Nonfiction: *The Flame Trees of Thika* (New York: Penguin Books, 1982), *On the Edge of the Rift* (New York: William Morrow, 1962), *With Forks and Hope* (New York: William Morrow, 1964), *Love Among the Daughters* (New York: William Morrow, 1968), *Out in the Midday Sun* (London: Chatto and Windus, 1985).

# Chapter 4
# Independence Era Mysteries

### Eugene Schleh

Independence began in Africa in the 1950s and surged in the 1960s. Overnight authority was passed over from colonial Europeans to Africans and the writing of mysteries followed the same transition. Some major African writers have tried the genre (e.g., Ngugi wa Thiongo and Cyprian Ekwensi) while numerous younger authors have moved into the field.

The Africa these writers, as well as European and American authors, portray is a continent in rapid change. Millions of Africans continue to live traditional, rural lives. But millions more have moved to the cities in search of jobs, or more accurately, of money. Many of these people can obtain only menial jobs such as the lawn men who cut grass with machetes (R)* or as servants. The only real change is that these people are more likely to be employed by Africans than by Europeans for Africans have moved into most of the positions of authority. For some time there are issues from the colonial era to clean up. Thus revenge for the "Mau Mau" killings in Kenya (H) or the massacre of a village during the revolution in Mozambique (D) can be central to mystery plots.

Other aspects of colonialism require resolution such as the expulsion of thousands of Asians who had settled in British East Africa (A, H).

*Text references are to the novels listed by letter in the accompanying bibliography.

Increasingly, however, the novels became more African and less European. The urban masses created new worlds, where urban crime and suffering thrived. Ross Thomas describes one city as "no sleepy African village. It was thirty square miles of wide-awake, vibrant, magnificent slum with all of a slum's cynical disregard for self-improvement. It was dirty, dog-eared urban sprawl, rotten at the core, and rotten at the edges" (R). While Ross' city is mythical, Dorothy Gilman describes Lusaka, Zambia as "full of thieves and spies" (G) and David Duchi has a character, almost proudly, describe Nairobi, Kenya as "not the Shangri-La the town operators told their clients. We had our share of muggers, murderers, pickpockets and crooks of all types and class. We had big time traffickers who would export their mothers in cans for cash. We had mafia type syndicates that ran everything from murder-for-hire to protection rackets" (E). Meja Mwanzi describes a character who has, in fact, joined the Mafia and "heads the first Mafia operation in East Africa," specializing in smuggling drugs, ivory, and diamonds from Tanzania and coffee from Uganda (N). These criminal pursuits seem to be oiled by universal corruption. "Who doesn't cheat in this country? The people in power. Top civil servants, contractors, judges, soldiers, policemen, pastors. Who doesn't cheat?" (J). Some authors seek external villains as the cause of their troubles. It is, for example, always easy to blame the South Africans or the white Rhodesians during their brief period of independence (M,P,O,G,Q). Kole Omotoso goes so far as to list nine countries he feels are already subverted and are "mere puppets of the apartheid governments" (P).

Most authors, however, seem almost proud that big-time crime is now in the hands of Africans. In Ross Thomas' *The Seersucker Whipsaw* an American public relations man is working for an African politician who is killed in a coup. When the American asks an involved military officer "Who backed you? The CIA— MI6?", the officer replies with modern Africa's position: "You give us far too little credit...Even Africans can sometimes manage their own affairs without the help of outsiders. It might be a lesson for you to learn" (R).

Indeed the Africans portrayed today, on both sides of the law, are often highly qualified. Among the mystery-solvers in recent novels, one can find a B.A. who turns private detective (J), a newsman with a B.A. from Harvard and a M.A. from Columbia (O), and a Ph.D. in Anthropology (P).

Today's Africans are also beginning to reverse the travel direction and rather than Europeans or Americans always coming to Africa some Africans are going abroad (C). Foreigners are also becoming more knowledgeable about Africa. The American who is frustrated at not finding big game in West Africa (R) is probably still in the majority, but more knowledgeable types are appearing. In an, at least, growing minority is a black American private detective created by Clifford Mason, who knows a man is lying when he used OBA as an Ashanti title (it is Nigerian), can tell a Zulu by the assagai (short spear) he is carrying, or thinks of a girl as "a high-cheek-boned, Fulani-type beauty" (M).

Africans are beginning to write detective/mystery fiction in rapidly growing numbers. Added to the foreigners who continue to use Africa as a setting, these authors should continue to provide a pleasant way for many to learn about the no-longer dark continent.

# Works Cited

A Anderson, John R.L. *Death in the Greenhouse.* New York: Charles Scribner's Sons, 1983.

B Blackburn, John. *Deep Among the Dead Men.* London: Jonathan Cape, 1973.

C Bleeck, Oliver. *The Brass Go-Between.* New York: William Morrow and Company, Inc., 1969.

D Driscoll, Peter. *The Barboza Credentials.* Philadelphia and New York: J.B. Lippincott Company, 1976.

E Duchi, David. *Assassins on Safari.* Nairobi: Longman Kenya Ltd., 1983.

F Ekwensi, Cyprian. *Yaba Round-About Murder.* Lagos: Tortoise Series Books, 1962.

G Gilman, Dorothy. *Mrs. Pollifax on Safari.* New York: Fawcett Crest, 1978.

H Huxley, Elspeth. *A Man from Nowhere.* London: Chatto & Windus, 1964.

I Ibizugbe, Uyi. *The Mysterious Ebony Carver.* Benin City, Nigeria: Ethiope Publishing Corporation, 1979.

J Ike, Chukwuemeka. *Expo '77.* Glasgow: Collins, 1980.

K   Knight, David. *Farquharson's Physique*. New York: Stein and Day, 1971.

L   MacLeod, Robert. *The Iron Sanctuary*. New York: Holt, Rinehart and Winston, 1966.

M   Mason, Clifford. *The Case of the Ashanti Gold*. New York: St. Martin's Press, 1985.

N   Mwangi, Meja. *The Bushtrackers*. Nairobi: Longman Kenya Ltd., 1979.

O   Ng'weno, Hilary. *The Man from Pretoria*. Nairobi: Longman Kenya Ltd., 1975.

P   Omotoso, Kole. *Fella's Choice*. Benin City, Nigeria: Ethiope Publishing Corporation, 1974.

Q   Thomas, Ross. *Cast A Yellow Shadow*. New York: The Mysterious Press, 1987.

R   _____ *The Seersucker Whipsaw*. New York: William Morrow & Company, Inc., 1967.

S   Woods, Sara. *Most Grievous Murder*. New York: St. Martin's Press, 1982.

# Chapter 5
# Popular Crime in Africa:
# The Macmillan Education Program

Mary Lou Quinn and Eugene P.A. Schleh

In the 1970s Macmillan Education began publishing a series of novels designed to meet the need for inexpensive, popular English-language literature throughout Africa. Each book includes the description: "All novels in the Macmillan Pacesetters series deal with contemporary issues and problems in a way that is particularly designed to interest young adults, although the stories are such that they will appeal to all ages." About one-third of the novels published thus far fall into the general category of crime fiction and these are the subject of this impressionistic paper.

Over two-thirds of the authors are Nigerian and Nigeria is also the country of largest sales (not surprising, perhaps, since something like one-fourth of all black Africans are Nigerian). "Pacesetters" do not achieve the sales of an Alistair MacLean best seller in America, but Table I shows they reach respectable levels and, significantly, continue to sell years after publication. Distribution is widespread. South Africa's position as the second best sales location reflects both a high level of literacy and rather surprising tolerance since South Africa is pretty safe to portray as a villain (e.g., *State Secret* and *The South African Affair*).

These novels provide both fascinating insights into contemporary Africa and evidence on the international interchange of popular culture. The Africa portrayed is one of a thin layer of the ultra-modern on a broad base of the traditional. Most Africans still live in rural settings and seldom appear in the Pacesetters. A "mammy wagon" may drive down a road crammed with passengers, animals, and goods or a roadside market may be visited with its myriad of goods—in very small scale. Traditional life appears most dramatically as a warped survival, such as elements of religion appearing in modern secret criminal societies which practice human sacrifice (E) or ritual murder (W). There is, however, an underlying superstition or faith in the old ways and beliefs that appear to be only common sense to the general population of these works. The Hausa of the Nigerian novels treat their tanwiji man with respect and go to him for advice. Voodooism is casually mentioned as we might mention Baptists and Catholicism. The customs and food favored by the leading characters are also traditional, such as a fine dish of pounded yams eaten with the fingers to give one a feeling of down home Africa.

**Sales 1985-87**

|  | Nigeria | Other West Africa | East & Central Africa | South Africa | All Other | Total |
|---|---|---|---|---|---|---|
| Mark of the Cobra (80) | 4,000 | 279 | 148 | — | 467 | 4,894 |
| Angel of Death (82) | 5,000 | 229 | 685 | 748 | 440 | 7,102 |
| State Secret (81) | 2,911 | 159 | 86 | 50 | 338 | 3,589 |
| Naira Power (82) | 12,000 | 164 | 142 | 870 | 499 | 13,675 |
| Black Temple (81) | 5,000 | 146 | 168 | — | 111 | 5,425 |
| Stop Press: Murder (83) | 5,000 | 329 | 139 | 1,125 | 390 | 6,983 |
| Border Runners (84) | 5,060 | 278 | 724 | 1,181 | 159 | 7,402 |
| The Lost Generation (85) | 60 | 430 | 1,040 | 980 | 40 | 2,550 |
| Too Young To Die (86) | 500 | 230 | 406 | 167 | 5 | 1,308 |
| Blackmailers (82) | 5,000 | 246 | 411 | 830 | 126 | 6,613 |
| Have Mercy (82) | 9,000 | 229 | 335 | 1,043 | 399 | 11,006 |
| Women For Sale (84) | 6,060 | 401 | 280 | 1,292 | 405 | 8,438 |
| Extortionist (83) | — | 181 | 131 | 865 | 381 | 1,558 |
| Coup! (82) | 3,000 | 159 | 402 | 925 | 372 | 4,858 |
| Cross Fire (82) | — | 259 | 575 | — | 424 | 1,258 |
| On the Road (80) | — | 129 | 532 | 900 | 412 | 1,973 |
| Smugglers (77) | — | 2,632 | 528 | 421 | 103 | 3,684 |
| South African Affair (82) | — | 366 | 139 | 376 | 490 | 1,371 |
| Dangerous Waters (84) | 5,060 | 902 | 763 | 970 | 125 | 7,820 |
| Money-Doublers (85) | 3,560 | 655 | 74 | 1,040 | 32 | 5,361 |
| The Instrument (80) | — | 1,124 | 230 | — | 72 | 1,426 |
| Stone of Vengeance (81) | — | 1,129 | 86 | 1,334 | 479 | 3,028 |

| The Worshippers | | | | | | |
|---|---|---|---|---|---|---|
| (79) | 3,000 | 129 | 104 | 400 | 154 | 3,787 |
| Finger of Suspicion | | | | | | |
| (84) | 8,000 | 521 | 225 | 1,405 | 472 | 10,623 |
| Dead of Night (83) | 2,000 | 1,184 | 252 | 600 | 380 | 4,416 |
| | 84,211 | 12,490 | 8,605 | 17,522 | 7,320 | 130,148 |

These aspects of African life show up in the general language and terminology used. Common adages such as "nobody owns up to eating with a lost knife" (D) are used to make points to the character who is more westernized. They also portray cultural customs as in the case of a Muslim wife who comments on the treatment of wives in general, "The broom a husband used in flogging the older wife is there on the top shelf waiting for the younger one." (D) The homiest touches come with little sayings that are full of local color. Giving a crocodile colic (G) or going after something like a fly goes after a ripe mango is not the kind of expression one would use in our everyday society. The use of local animal traits to describe people is something relatively common to most peoples; however, the choice of animals helps zero in on the area the expression is coming from. We might make a comment such as "that person is a real dog" or "he is a wolf." In Africa more readily used examples might be, fast as a mamba, "as sure as a mouse could tell cheese from butter," (A) and strong as a lion, blind as a rhino. There might also be a slight twist to a western saying such as "a mad elephant in a glass shop" rather than a bull in a china shop. (H)

For the most part, however, these books are about the most modern of Africans; those who either have lived abroad or at least, eagerly follow European and American culture. Their tastes are elitist and would, in fact, probably make most Westerner's envious. Heroes and villains alike do not just smoke cigarettes, they smoke Benson and Hedges. They do not drink local liquors, they drink Remy Martin cognac, champagne, and Chevas Regal (N,Q,O,A). Most visibly they are car crazy. While one hero does drive a jalopy affectionately nicknamed Jezebel (V,W,X,Y), most characters spread their business around the globe and Subarus, Volvos, Datsuns, Peugeots, and Volks abound. At the top of the scale are infrequent American cars like an "enormous" Thunderbird (W) or a Dodge driven by killers. Most often, to the envy of these readers, both good guys and villains zoom around in Mercedes (familiarly known as Mercy Bensons) (V). The most extreme case of automotive consumption occurs in Alily's *Mark of the Cobra* where the hero alternates between a Volvo 244 GLE, a Mercedes, and a silver Volks SP2 while the chief villain has a garage with a white convertible E-type Jaguar, a gold plated Rolls-Royce Corniche, and a platinum Jensen Intercepter III.

It is suggested that the proliferation of automobiles in the urban areas is enormous. One book describes the horrible traffic in Lagos and official action to control it by restricting driving to odd and even numbered days depending on the last digit of one's license plate. African ingenuity (and a booming economy) foil the plan, however, as people just rush out and acquire a second car so they can have one even license number and one odd (D).

The use of automobiles in very descriptive ways sometimes leads to trouble. One wonders with all the cars being driven around Africa, how many are chauffered. Many of the characters have drivers just as it is common practice to have house boys no matter how tiny your living quarters or how small your income. When a writer wishes to write about the role of his hero but is not used to driving or maintaining his own car, certain discrepancies crop up. This was the case in two books when car maintenance was being discussed. In preparing his car for a long and dangerous trip, the hero made sure he checked the oil and filled the *carburetor* with water (C). The second instance was pressing down the clutch pedal in an automatic so that a high speed chase would be successful. Traces of British influence are also evident in the terminology used with cars. The term saloon car is quite often used and in discussing parts of a car, bonnet instead of hood, and boot rather than trunk, are used.

The enormous wealth available is very unevenly distributed which leads to tremendous pressure to survive. The Nigerian books, in particular, suggest that corruption at all levels is rampant and accepted with resignation. Payoffs to get a hotel room are essential because "This was still Nigeria" (O). Police at all levels must be bribed on an almost daily basis (N,G,L) and high government officials are different only in that they deal with larger amounts (G,V) and are known as "the naira swallowers." Not even the military who seized power in part to halt corruption, are exempt (W). The overriding philosophy in almost every Nigerian book and in some of the West African novels can be summed up in the quote: "In Nigeria, when you have money you are something and when you don't have it you are nothing." (E) Even the title of one book, *Naira Power*, states the case very bluntly.

The common man in the street has little recourse; he must go with the system—and try to get his. Violent crime, however, is a different story. Here the people can act for themselves. Traditionally, it is suggested, crowds in Muslim Kano might stone a drunk to death (F). Now the technique is modernized. The cry of "Thief" quickly gathers a vigilante mob and if the miscreant is caught instant justice is dispensed in the form of an auto tire around the body, a dose of petrol and immediate cremation.

Against such a turbulent background the writers present a fascinating array of villains and heroes (and heroines), usually of the most modern type and often owing an obvious debt to Western popular culture influence. Villains range from the mundane, such as government officials who smuggle prostitutes from neighboring countries, (L) to the much more exotic. There is a definite liking for organized crime with descriptive names: "The Brotherhood of Hope" (drug smugglers, V), "The Black Gang" (mostly white men in varied international crime, B), "The Black Temple" (smugglers, E), or "The Crusaders" (high government types, F). Most of the criminals are strictly indigenous although one book does bring in white men with Italian names for heroin smuggling (G) and several make use of the favorite foreign enemy, South Africa, either obliquely (F) or very centrally in the form of mercenaries (R) or agents of B.O.S.S. (The Bureau of State Security) (C,R).

Above the organizations are talented individuals, sometimes with descriptive nom de guerre: "Brains" and "Worldman" (P), "The Scorpion" (M) or "The Cobra" (A). But not only villains and heroes are known by their nicknames; some of the lesser characters also carry nicknames. One example that shows a western influence is that of a Karate instructor known as the "Black Bionic Man." (H)

The novelists are frank about the debt they owe for some of the villains and the crimes they engage ·in. One has government officials inspiring themselves with a private showing of Marlon Brando in *The Godfather* (N). Readers may suspect a greater influence and take lightly one hero's disclaimer that he is not James Bond (V). The debt to Fleming is made explicit by "The Cobra" who explains to the hero that he gained his ambition to be a world-class villain by reading Fleming, especially *Live and Let Die*, and modeled himself on Bond's enemies (A).

The hero facing The Cobra is himself an obvious African take-off of Bond. Jack Ebony (originally Abani) is huge, a martial arts expert and one of only two surviving agents of the Nigerian Naval Department's Officer of Special Strategic Service (OS3) with a license to kill. Another hero is the former head of SATAN (Squad Against Terrorism and Nefarious acts) (M). Policemen or former policemen appear frequently (F,O,V,W,X,Y). Victor Thorpe's recurring hero, Paul Okoro, is a journalist with a bit of a limp (since he lost much of one leg to a crocodile in a ritual murder attempt in his first adventure). He is also accompanied by and eventually marries an extraordinary woman, Aimie, a lawyer.

Extraordinary fits the description of many of the women in these African Mysteries. In the cultural climate of male dominance, it is the woman in the story who comes up with the workable plans of action and could be called the brains of the operation.

There are several classifications of the women's roles in African society depending on the religious background as well as country or area they come from and whether or not they are a Europeanized "been to." It is apparently not uncommon for husbands to bring their wives from the 'north' (as in Nigeria) and set them up as the bread winners in the business of prostitution, just until they can get their feet under them and some form of stable employment. This arrangement is portrayed as being an acceptable practice of using resources without many of the ugly overtones of pimps and cruel clients. It can, however, be the subject of corrupted practices when not on a husband, wife relationship plane (L).

In many of the stories prostitutes and bordellos are as common a backdrop as fast food joints in the United States, and are visited and the wares sampled as casually as ordering a cheeseburger.

From this description it would be easy to assume that the women of Africa are simple and submissive objects to the men of Africa, but this would be a western interpretation. The effect is surprisingly different. The men in many of these mysteries, who are drawn to the women, are either in trouble, unable to make a living or just have trouble coping with society. They are in need of direction or ideas to help solve a mystery, and the women are the right source!

In Okpi's book *Coup!*, the leading man, detective Jetas, is actually led by Major Azarea Mandingo, a woman in a top ranking security position. She is extremely capable and at least three steps ahead of Jetas all the time. There seems to be no unwritten law that says women cannot operate complicated electronics equipment or heavy armaments in tough physical situations. With an Armalite Automatic cradled in her arms, Major Mandingo kicks open a door and is ready to take out the villains as smoothly as any male detective. In her fast thinking she realizes that to survive in the situation that she and Jetas have found themselves, they must leave the country after they have done their duty. She is prepared with getaway money and her passport. Jetas is left stumbling to catch up with her thinking as she patiently explains the facts of life to him.

The one irony in this story surrounds the code names of some of the characters. In this case the head of the government that Major Mandingo is protecting is called Topdog while her code name is simply Female One. Although it is obvious to the reader who the directing force is, often the male characters are oblivious to the capabilities of the females. The women are courageous and have a logical and common sense ability to figure out what is going on and what can be done about it. They are the thinkers. They have learned how to use the system, hold power, and for the most part are able to survive.

Survival is a subject of another phenomenon in these African mysteries which is somewhat different from western traditions. Very often the key female figure, who has helped the leading man throughout the book, will be eliminated in the end. The African novelist is not at all squeamish about having a woman shot dead as part of the wrap-up or cleanup of the story. Many times part of the suspense of these books comes from wondering if and when leading women will wind up dead. In one story (A) we are introduced in great detail to a lovely and intelligent agent. A budding relationship develops between her and the leading male agent but then in a flash of a paragraph she is struck down by a giant cobra which she manages to kill before she dies. The reader might assume that this will become the motive for revenge on the part of the leading man but instead her character is quickly forgotten. This scenario can be best compared with the James Bond stories but it is done so quickly as to come as a shock to the reader.

The Pacesetter's crime fiction could be categorized in a number of ways. There are international plots with the villains coming from outside the country and working with easily corruptible elements within the state. These books have the most James Bond flavor because the state is saved by the lone agent with the help, acknowledged or not, of a woman. Kalu Okpi is one of the main authors of this fiction with *The South African Affair* and *On The Road*. These stories are remarkable for the weapons and military at the disposal of a long agent who, with a phone call, can call up the country's air force to do his bidding. There is no acknowledgement of the bureaucratic red tape frustration that is characteristic in the western version of this genre.

Running underneath these crime fiction books in an often subtle way is the ever present possibility, or consequences, of a government overthrow. Again, Kalu Okpi brings this to the forefront of his book, *Coup!*. Stories such as *The Border Runners* point up the consequences of ever changing governments that make blackmarketing and smuggling profitable, as well as dangerous, since the new governments have their own military forces out for a piece of the action. The reader is all too aware of the instability of even the most innocuous daily routines. In *The Extortionist* it is evident that a government could be easily toppled without planning to do so simply by the actions of a greedy organized crime boss.

There is a difference in the respect given to the police forces of the African countries in which the stories are set. Books set in Nigeria portray the police as being generally incompetent, poorly educated and on the take. In Kenya the police are taken more seriously as a crime fighting unit and some stories are almost police procedural in nature. In Omondi Makoloo's *Too Young To Die*, he states this concept in very concrete terms. "This is Kenya. The cops here are sharp." (p. 42)

For young readers there are many societal problems which are addressed along with a crime or mystery, a category of social and criminal injustice. The educational system is often the target of this fiction. The pressures of students to pass the examination and board appointments in order to continue their education is almost inconceivable to students in the United States. The ability to get a job and to simply live hinges on going through the educational system. Fathers will bribe officials with money and favors, sell their daughter's favors and even kill to obtain an appointment for their offspring. Education is a pay-as-you-go system and stories tell of all manner of crimes committed just to save money to pay for school. With that certificate of secondary graduation the student is almost guaranteed a position in the government, which handles almost every aspect of life with a ministry of one sort or another. There is no moralizing about this being wrong but there is a note of concern and desire for change.

These novels open a window on to a culture that is very different from most western cultures. The society seems to be broken down into three distinct groups: government workers, who have fringe benefits of housing and transportation; tribal life, which is rarely mentioned; and the very large criminal element. Because the latter group makes up such a large percentage of the character population, it is not uncommon to have books depicting rival gang warfare. Organized crime is not the same as the 'Mafia' but more on the order of a chief heading a large gang with government officials being paid off. The gang is taken care of but the chief, much like the government, takes care of its ministers.

Occasionally the young people become the main characters in plots. *The Lost Generation, Secret Revenge,* and *The Ebony Carver* all feature young people out to fix an injustice or make the world a better place. They generally work in groups of several boys and one girl, although in *The Lost Generation* the main characters are a boy and a girl. The girl, Cecilia, is out to avenge the murder of her father by a gang of thieves. Using cunning and ingenuity as well as her looks, she finally confronts the killers in a dark park without benefit of a weapon. The boy, Wanyonyi, has been irresistibly attracted to Cecilia, and in trying to find out more about her, he is caught up in her plot to catch the murderers. He is exposed to a lesson which Cecilia wishes to teach him about what happens to "nice boys...roaming, neglecting their studies" and being led astray by bad influences. Wanyonyi is shown that it is best to remain quiet, creative and innocent.

In a different twist of events, *Sweet Revenge* sees a group of students band together to go after a construction company that is corrupt and using inferior materials which cause the death of a fellow student and the wreck of their new school buildings. The ever present effects of widespread corruption are brought to light in this book and a majority of the other books. Murder, theft and prostitution are all seen as by-products of corruption which has become a natural way of life.

The contradictions evidenced in these works along with the thought patterns, modes of speech, social settings, and consumables all leave their special glimpses of a fascinating and unique variety of cultures. Like a detective, the western reader fits the pieces of the cultural jigsaw puzzle together in order to grasp a clearer picture of an unknown society, and, like a mystery, one is drawn further into an exciting investigation of new people and places.

It is exciting to experience the birth and growth of a culture's literature and also somewhat sad to recognize western influences. But the special way in which these influences are adapted to African society increases one's fascination with the whole process of African Mystery genre.

# Works Cited

Bibliography of Pacesetters Used
(Published in London and Basingstoke)

A  Alily, Valentine, *Mark of the Cobra*, 1980.
B  Dlovu, Aanoi, *Angle of Death*, 1982.
C  Dube, Hope, *State Secret*, 1981.
D  Emecheta, Buchi, *Naira Power*, 1982.
E  Garba, Mohmed Tukur, *The Black Temple*, 1981.
F  ———. *Stop Press: Murder*, 1983.
G  Irungu, James and Shimanyula, James, *The Border Runners*, 1984.
H  Irungu, James, *The Lost Generation*, 1985.
I  Makoloo, Omondi, *Too Young To Die*, 1986.
J  Mangut, Joseph, *The Blackmailers*, 1982.
L  ——— *Have Mercy*, 1982.
M  ——— *Women For Sale*, 1984.
N  Nwokolo, Chuma, *The Extortionist*, 1983.
O  ——— *Cross-fire!*, 1982.
P  ——— *On The Road*, 1980.
Q  ——— *The Smugglers*, 1977.
R  ——— *The South African Affair*, 1982.
S  Phil-Ebosie, Philip, *Dead of Night*, 1983.
T  Sotabinda, Maurice, *Dangerous Waters*, 1984.
U  ——— *The Money-Doublers*, 1985.
V  Thorpe, Victor, *The Exterminators*, 1987.
W  ——— *The Instrument*, 1980.
X  ——— *Stone of Vengeance*, 1981.
Y  ——— *The Worshippers*, 1979.
Z  Umelo, Rosina, *Finger of Suspicion*, 1984.

# Chapter 6
# Africa in West German Crime Fiction

## Dieter Riegel

The new German crime novel, going back to the mid-sixties, has established a reputation as a realistic social novel critical of contemporary West German society. Normally plots are set in West Germany, but occasionally authors venture into other countries. They either follow the escape routes of their criminals, or observe German tourists on vacation abroad. Lately, some authors have set their plots in Africa or have used African characters visiting West Germany.

African themes in crime novels reflect a growing awareness of Africa in West Germany. Contributing to this interest in Africa are the recognition of the increased political importance of Third World countries, expansion of commercial ties with Africa, the ongoing public debate about the pros and cons of development aid as well as more interest in Africa as an exotic vacation destination.

Throughout the fifties and sixties West Germans calmly observed the process of decolonization that took place in Africa. After all, West Germany had no stake in colonialism. The 30 odd years of German colonial rule in Africa that came to an end in 1918 due to the First World War were only a dim memory. It was also 'conveniently' forgotten that throughout the Weimar Republic and the Nazi period nationalists had bemoaned the loss of the colonies as yet another of the injustices perpetrated against Germany by the Versailles treaty.

It is not surprising that in spite of the renewed interest in Africa the perception of this continent is still largely marked by ignorance of contemporary realities, by longstanding prejudices, and by false myths (Paeffgen 495).

The myth of the white man's superiority predates German colonial rule. It is a testimony to the ethnocentric view of other races prevalent in 18th and 19th century Europe. Viewed as exotic, sensuous beings and considered anthropologically inferior to the Europeans black Africans were judged not in their own right but in terms of European values (Sadji, U. 280). When the Germans colonized Africa, their colonial literature justified their intrusion as fulfillment of a mission to bring civilization to the 'natives', and to teach them the value of work and discipline (Oguntoye 34; Ridley 385). Throughout the Weimar Republic and the Nazi regime the right of the stronger to dominate the weaker was defended in the propaganda aimed at regaining possession of the former colonies (Sadji, A. B. 54-58). Even in the early seventies attitudes about Africa were still marked by condescension or expressions of paternalistic good will towards Black Africa. (Paeffgen 498).

A good example of paternalistic attitudes towards blacks can be seen in a novel by Louis Weinert-Wilton. He published a series of crime novels in the late twenties and early thirties in the style of Edgar Wallace. Most of them are still in print. He features a strong good-natured and loyal negro named Bob who appears on the scene when the protagonist requires help. He speaks a hackneyed German, is obedient, cheerful and proud to help his master.

In novels set in Africa, authors typically catapult an outsider, mostly a West German, into an African country. This stratagem allows for critical comparisons of Germany with the African country chosen.

Detlef Wolff's *Katenkamp in Kenia* (1983; *Katenkamp in Kenya*) is set in a country which is considered a tourist paradise by adventurous West Germans. The author, born in 1934, is a journalist from Bremen. He wrote successful detective novels featuring the Hamburg police investigator Katenkamp. In this novel, the eighth in the series, Katenkamp has an assignment in Kenya. He is to give a three-week course in modern investigation techniques at the Police school in Nairobi. On his arrival at the airport in Mombasa he is met by a local colleague, Assistant Superintendent Azhar

Shikuku, who has two unresolved murder cases on his hands, one involving a German tourist. Katenkamp is asked for help, reluctantly consents, and is immediately whisked off to Mombasa Police Headquarters to start the investigation.

Detlef Wolff makes good use of his first-hand knowledge of contemporary Kenya, provides local flavour, is informative, and has a sympathetic view of the country. At the same time he is keenly aware of the nefarious effect of European 'civilisation' on Kenya, particularly the devastating consequences of tourism, an important economic factor, on the social fabric and values of Kenya. This is the major theme developed at different levels of the novel.

By using a third-person narrative perspective, Wolff creates the opportunity of expressing a variety of social commentary in different settings by revealing the thoughts of major and minor characters.

Katenkamp is the most obvious character to mirror Wolff's own experience of Kenya. He is the visiting outsider, but not the typical tourist. He has come to work and views the German tourists who arrived on the same plane critically and at times with disgust. Already at the airport he overhears impatient tourists complain about the slow pace of immigration controls. Jokingly they threaten to show the "negroes" "what Prussian discipline is" (14). Katenkamp is sensitive to such remarks that attest to the continuation of racial arrogance among Germans.

During his stay in Mombasa Katenkamp is struck by the fact that the European tourists live in a world apart from real Africa. The luxurious hotels, the beaches are their domain. They attract crowds of the poor who want to benefit from their 'wealth.' At times Katenkamp feels he might as well be at the Costa Brava so little 'African' can he discern in the artificial surroundings created for the tourists. He searches for the authentic but elusive Africa, occasionally catching a glimpse of it. He is unable to reconcile the stark contrast between the "parade of poverty" he observes in the streets with the false world of tourism.

Most intriguing in Wolff's novel is the professional co-operation between a Kenyan and German police officer. Although Katenkamp has come to teach Africans about modern police work he quickly discovers that he can learn much about investigation methods from his Kenyan colleague. To boot, he gets a lesson about the real Africa.

Shikuku, a down-to-earth, clever and experienced professional, is successful in his work because he is aware of the mentality and social conditions of Kenyans and is capable of applying his insights. It is not surprising that he is skeptical about the course that Katenkamp is to give in Nairobi. Although his government develops and encourages tourism Shikuku does not think much of it. His experience as a police officer has abundantly shown him that it creates too many problems. Throughout the story Shikuku points out to Katenkamp the negative social consequences of international tourism. The enclaves of well-off tourists represent a temptation to poor Kenyans. Consequences are corruption and prostitution. This has the greatest effect on young women from rural areas who are lured into the city where they often fall in the hands of pimps and work as prostitutes in the bars frequented by tourists. Such women often become estranged from their native villages, with infanticide as a typical crime resulting from the tourist industry.

Katenkamp shares Shikuku's disapproval of tourism. He sees the demeaning aspects of a situation that produces too many social parasites who are either begging or try to sell something. He remembers the German postwar experience: "After the war Germans must have appeared to the American soldiers like that. Tourists as a kind of occupation force" (133; author's translation).

Shikuku's and Katenkamp's co-operation is not entirely harmonious, but certainly productive and leads to the discovery of the murderer. They divide up their tasks in such a way that each can use their special expertise. Katenkamp is to interview the German-speaking witnesses, while Shikuku takes care of the Africans. From time to time they discuss their findings or interview witnesses jointly.

One victim, a German tourist, was found on a hotel compound under a palm tree, apparently struck by a falling coconut. This soon is shown to be a murder, and, according to Shikuku, committed by a white person, since an African would never have made the mistake of placing the wrong kind of coconut under the tree. Similarly, when at a later stage someone tries to assassinate

Katenkamp, Shikuku concludes that it must have been a white, since Africans do not normally have the means to buy shoes or a gun. Altogether Shikuku points out to Katenkamp that murder motives in Kenya are small in number: apart from infanticide murders are either committed for monetary gain or out of jealousy.

The other victim is a young African prostitute murdered on the premises of a club on the same night as the other victim. The latter had previously promised to take her over to Germany where she would earn a lot more money working in a bar.

In both cases the number of suspects is quickly narrowed down to two German tourists, Ingo Hesselbach and Carmen Pötsche who both had arrived from Hamburg along with the man murdered subsequently.

The solution of the mystery reveals that the male murder victim, Peter Texel, had come to Kenya to find another African prostitute to replace the one who had been killed because she had become a nuisance. Her passport was to get the new prostitute out of Kenya. The investigation ends with the revelation that Hesselbach had committed both murders, that of Texler, because he had a conflict with him about the smuggling of drugs, that of the prostitute because he hated blacks.

As in his earlier novels Wolff critically examines the conduct of police officers. Katenkamp learns a great deal about crime in Africa from Shikuku but disapproves of some of his investigative techniques, particularly the use of violence to intimidate witnesses. At the same time Katenkamp is well aware of the violence perpetrated by the German police when dealing with demonstrators. No less serious is Katenkamp's discovery that Shikuku takes bribes from a bar owner who thus can operate a drug smuggling racket unmolested by the police. Shikuku justifies himself by saying that corruption is part of the system.

D. Wolff, like Katenkamp, sees Kenya as a "disturbed" country not yet recovered from the ravages of colonialism. Tourism is seen to be a continuation of the harmful European influence that has detrimental repercussions on the value system of society. Wolff offers a critical view of Kenyan society with corruption visible at all levels.

These negative aspects are seen as a perversion. The real Africa, however, hidden and under siege, is still alive.

In addition to providing an illustration of the harmful influence of tourism, the murder mystery serves as a medium to criticize West Germany as well. However corrupt Shikuku might be Katenkamp is much more deeply disturbed by the revelation that the murderer Hesselkamp belongs to an organization that wants to eradicate negroes. The inhumanity of a new fascism is contrasted with African crime which is more "human" because it stems from need and poverty.

In Christine Grän's *Weisse sterben selten in Samyana* (1986; *Whites seldom die in Samyana*) a more comprehensive account of the relationship between Africa and West Germany is presented. Christine Grän, now a freelance journalist in Bonn, draws on her five years stay in Botswana as manager of a bush restaurant. She sets her novel in fictitious Samyana, a country sandwiched between South Africa and Mozambique. Her protagonist is a woman, the journalist Anna Marx, who is sent to Samyana to write an article about the murder of Anna Hellmann, the wife of a German expert stationed in the capital to help develop the tourists industry.

Before leaving, Anna Marx is briefed about Samyana by a representative of the Bonn Ministry for Economic Co-operation, a ministry charged with co-ordinating and supporting development aid projects in Third World countries. She does not find out much more than that West Germany is only marginally involved; a few agricultural projects in the interior and a fish plant project. Four German experts are stationed in the capital Basuto, a doctor, two economists, and tourism advisor Hellmann, whose wife had been murdered.

Much more revealing are the comments about Africa that come her way from the moment she accepts the assignment to go to Samyana. Still back home in Bonn, a fellow journalist lectures her on South Africa and ventures the predication that as soon as Africans take over South Africa they would begin to kill each other (like everywhere else) and ruin the country. Once on African soil, her first contacts are Europeans. An Englishman points out the social problems caused by overpopulation. He bemoans the ugly architecture, the lack of urban planning and makes adverse comments about the Africans who only live for the day without regard for the future. Later, one of the German experts explains to her that whites in Africa generally lack the capacity to react to Africa and the Africans in a 'normal' manner, but rather tend towards extreme positions: the racists, who always find their prejudices confirmed, the liberals, who don't care as long as they can live well and can do some good, and the Afrophiles, who find everything beyond criticism (33).

In researching her story, Anna Marx soon becomes acquainted with Embassy staff and members of the small German community who each have a specific view of Africans. The German Ambassador and his wife hate Africa, consider Africans unreliable, and development aid futile. German experts offer contradictory views about the best way of assisting a developing country like Samyana. The agriculture expert believes the standard of living can be raised by improvement of land use methods whereas the medical expert insists that birth control is the ultimate solution.

Hellmann, the tourism expert, has a more skeptical view. He deplores that financial aid is misused to further the interests of the elite with the result that the condition of the poor becomes even more hopeless. Another expert dreams of creating a progressive school system but he overlooks the fact that basic education is needed.

Whatever their opinions might be, all these experts have in common that they live a luxurious life away from the people they are supposed to help.

The murdered Anna Hellmann, however, attempted to take Africans seriously and treated them as equals. Her unorthodox behavior towards Africans was considered offensive by the Europeans as well as by the African elite. No wonder that an African, who worked as gardner at the Hellmanns, became the prime suspect. He was arrested and imprisoned despite having an alibi.

The relationship between Anna Marx and Police Chief Mnusi is at the center of the story. Both have an interest in finding out the truth about the murder. Mnusi is under political pressure to solve the case quickly, since the murder of a white person is hurting the prestige of the country. Yet Mnusi is fully aware that he cannot conduct a fair investigation because white suspects enjoy a de facto privileged position.

Anna Marx is allowed to visit the imprisoned suspect who convinces her that he is not a murderer. She therefore continues to investigate the case on her own, and in the process learns a lot about the real Africa.

Her understanding of Africa is deepened as the result of visiting a medicineman in a village. Rumours about a ritual murder had spread in town and she wanted to investigate whether there existed any connection to the case at hand.

Anna is accompanied by Percy Molefe, secretary of the President's wife. Educated in Oxford, he despises the old Samyana, yet has somewhat lost his belief in progress. He is estranged from the traditions of his country and only feels at ease among the African elite. Yet in spite of his enlightened views he is secretly afraid of the medicineman, this last representative and guardian of the old Africa with its traditions and rites.

The medicineman declares that the white woman was murdered by a white man and warns her to be careful since she will get very close to the murderer.

The medicineman's pronouncements turn out to be correct. Anna Marx discovers almost by chance that the murder has been committed by the Ambassador. In a tense scene he admits his guilt to Anna. But the real inner drama of the novel occurs prior to that scene when Anna was still in the dark about the identity of the murderer. Called back to Bonn Anna pays a last visit to Police Chief Mnusi, who in the meantime had solved the case in his own particular way. In order to save his job he gave in to political pressure and decided to hand the accused black gardener over to the courts after having destroyed his alibi with a little bit of help. Anna Marx, at first appalled at the thought that an innocent man might be hanged, in the end recognizes Mnusi's dilemma. To arrest a white suspect without undisputable proof would have been impossible for Mnusi on account of the political repercussions of such an act. Instead of standing up for the truth he had decided to conclude the case in the most expedient manner.

Anna Marx is reluctant to condemn Mnusi: she thinks of the many compromises she had consented to in her journalistic work, and she was not sure how she would react if her editor insisted on her writing a story that was not true: "Everywhere people were weak, corrupt, cowards" (123; author's translation).

Christine Grän presents an African country full of contradictions. Her protagonist tries to experience it without prejudice. Anna Marx, like Wolff's Katenkamp, witnesses corruption among the African elite. But her criticism is tempered by the knowledge that Germans have similar failures.

This cautious approach is also evident in the plot structure. In both novels the murderers are Germans who don't care about or even hate Africa. Both Grän and Wolff are skeptical about the usefulness of development aid, yet are at a loss to propose alternatives. They are, however, successful in conveying interesting information about contemporary Africa, and both condemn racial arrogance.

Henry Kolarz, born in 1927, set two of his novels in Africa. *Kalahari* (1979; *Kalahari*) is a political thriller featuring an episode from the guerrilla struggle for majority rule in Zimbabwe. Most of the action, however, takes place in Botswana, where a newly arrived young German aid worker is involuntarily mixed up in the liberation struggle. Dieter Hahn has to deliver a truck in Maun and takes a detour through the Kalahari. On his way he meets an African who later turns out to be Tutuma, leader of the Zimbabwe liberation army. Tutuma had just completed a daring mission stealing diamonds from the Orapa mine intended as payment for weapons from the Soviet Union.

On the run from South African agents, Tutuma becomes friends with the German aid worker. He is also hounded by Feuchtenheimer, the South African security chief of the Orapa mine, who had been blackmailed to reveal the date of the diamond transport. Feuchtenheimer is on a personal vendetta, not so much to recover the diamonds but to save his own position which he is in danger of losing as long as Tutuma is alive and able to reveal Feuchtenheimer's betrayal.

Feuchtenheimer's several attempts to kill Tutuma fail, and in the end he is murdered himself.

Like the other authors, Kolarz uses the opportunity to provide interesting information about the country, the natural habitat, the people and their traditions. He introduces a Herero family who still master a few words of German, a reminder of the German colonial past in Africa.

The figure of the German aid worker allows Kolarz to broach the topic of development aid, which he treats with considerably less skepticism than Wolff and Grän. Dieter Hahn has come to Botswana to help the Africans and make amends for the injustices the whites had done in Africa. He is on his way to establish a brigade which will help Africans help themselves. From a German colleague in Maun who has already supervised a brigade successfully for a few years he hears some words of criticism: the Africans don't seem to understand the value of work and necessity for producing more than they need themselves. Another point of criticism is the political interference of local dignitaries who exploit the aid projects for their own financial gain.

Dieter Hahn is, however, undisturbed. He takes to heart the advice the President of the Federal Republic of Germany had given to an assembly of Third World aid workers: "Even if I know that I cannot achieve anything, I will nevertheless try again and again" (303; author's translation).

In Kolarz' other African-based novel *Die roten Elefanten* (1981; *The Red Elefants*) the element of detection plays a more important role. The novel is set in Kenya with the African Adipo as the major protagonist, charged by the government with establishing a Mobile Anti-Poaching Strike Unit to enforce the four year old ban on hunting and marketing of trophies.

Adipo assembles a team of Africans and Europeans. Among them is the German Karl Wegner. He had been a professional hunter in Kenya for 17 years. He now returns to Kenya, after an absence of four years he had spent in Germany selling safaris to tourists. Kolarz makes it clear that this operation is run by an African. The Europeans are subordinates and accept their role, as is illustrated by the example of Wegner, who in his career as a hunter used to be in charge of Adipo. Kolarz shows that this team with members of different ethnic backgrounds is capable of harmonious co-operation in the difficult task of tracking down the leaders of an organization that illegally exports trophies and is responsible for the slaughter of protected animals.

Adipo and his colleagues use a variety of detection techniques normally encountered in detective novels. The criminals, however, initially go unpunished, since influence at the political level protects them from prosecution. Kolarz points at Kenyatta's widow as the force behind this type of organized crime. The book suggest, though, that eventually, she will lose the status of untouchability.

Kolarz concerns himself in these two novels with crimes perpetrated in and against Africa. Africans, Kolarz seems to suggest, have to learn to protect themselves and take their affairs in their own hands.

Erich Loest's novel *Waffenkarussel (Weapons Roundabout)* was first published in 1968 in the German Democratic Republic under the pseudonym Hans Wallmann. It appeared in West Germany in 1986 for the first time under his real name. Loest had been imprisoned for political reason and was allowed to publish again in 1966. He wrote a series of detective novels with the London Police Inspector George Varnay. He published them under a pseudonym for easier access to a publishing house. In *Weapons Roundabout* a murder committed in London points to an illegal weapons export racket. Varnay decides to travel to Nigeria by boat in the hope of finding more clues during the voyage. Someone tries to assassinate him and he is hospitalized in Dakar. On his return to London he finds out that the mysterious murder case could have political repercussions for Britain. Varnay travels to Nigeria a second time, this time under the auspices of the British Secret Service. He is promptly arrested in Nigeria, but is later released.

The plot is set against the political turmoil that lead to the bloody civil war. At the same time the fierce competition between British and European weapons dealers is revealed. They are only too willing to supply weapons to the Nigerian opposition, which is represented by Tschukuma, Vice-Governour of the province of Kano.

The presence of a German military advisor is of interest. Bergmüller secretly trains recruits who will be available for the uprising planned by Tschukuma. Bergmüller was a highly decorated officer in the Hitler army. After the war he used his military expertise in various troublespots of the world fighting against bolshevism. His attitude towards Africans is not racist but rather is ideologically motivated. Thus he can claim to have friends among negroes and is willing to concede that there are many cultured blacks, although mainly in countries governed by rightwing regimes. But otherwise he shares the prejudice that blacks lack diligence and discipline, virtues that he teaches his recruits in Nigeria.

Acts of piracy committed against German ships along the West African coast prompted Frankfurt author Heribert Bauer, who uses the pseudonym Harry Porter, to write *Todestrip nach Afrika* (*Deathtrip to Africa*), published in 1987 in the dime novels series *Kommissar X*. The protagonist, New York private eye Jo Walker, is asked by a German shipping agency to investigate a recent attack on a German vessel in the harbour of Abidjan, Ivory Coast. As is usual in dime novels, the emphasis is on action, and Jo Walker goes after the criminals with gusto. He succeeds in eliminating the gang leaders, an Englishman and an African who had drifted in from some other African country. The novel shows that the success of the well armed gangsters is in part due to information received from corrupt officials. Although Jo Walker co-operates with African policemen, the reader is given very little insight into the social conditions that lead to crime in this country.

African themes are occasionally used in German settings. Norbert Klugmann's and Peter Mathews' *Flieg, Adler Kühn* (1985; *Fly, Eagle Kühn*) is the third in a series of unique satirical, humorous novels. Two Kenyans, Henry and Gabriel, have come to Germany to denounce a German chemical company that produces a pesticide abundantly sprayed in Kenya's coffee plantations and the cause of disease and even loss of human life. At first they try to inform the public about the use of this deadly poison in Kenya by talking to people in coffee shops or at bus stops, but without much success.

The 'natives' are sympathetic, but are not in the mood to stop enjoying their coffee because of some disaster in a far-away country they know little about.

In an ironic reversal of stereotypes the Africans finally come to the conclusion that whites are like children, innocent and cruel, and with a good conscience at that. Their meetings with company officials are equally unsuccessful.

At that point they initiate a 'terrorist' action by spraying the company's poison on the plants kept in the company's offices, thus creating mass hysteria. Also the media suddenly get interested in the issue. In addition, Gabriel and Henry use 'voodoo' to harm company officials and finally achieve their objective: closing of the company's branch plant in Kenya.

Klugmann and Mathews offer little information about Kenya, rather their aim is to expose the apathy of Germans toward the disastrous effects of the activities of profit-oriented industries in Third World countries.

In general, German authors have a positive and understanding attitude toward their fictional African characters. When it comes to political leaders, however, criticism of Africans is more direct and blunt, as is the case in Felix Huby's story "Leibwache" (1988; "Bodyguard"). Huby, born in 1938, published in the last decade a successful series of novels with the Stuttgart police inspector Ernst Bienzle as the series figure. In this story Bienzle is responsible for the security of a visiting African dictator. Bienzle does not hide his animosity towards the official guest who is seen as a murderer, and exploiter of his people. In a visit to a modern sewage treatment plant, a nephew tries to assassinate the dictator. Ironically, Bienzle saves the dictator's life. In doing so he pushes him into a smelly basin.

This farcical ending cannot, however, compensate the lack of a political concept to deal with dictatorship. Huby points out that the politicians are well aware of the immorality of the African ruler's regime, yet they are willing to co-operate with him, because German industry needs certain raw material from this country.

A more sophisticated approach to political and moral issues is taken by Peter Schmidt in his novel *Die Stunde des Geschichtenerzählers*(1987; *The Hour of the Storyteller*). Schmidt, born in 1944, has a number of highly acclaimed polit-thrillers to his credit. In the novel, Diana Hirsch, a young historian from the island of Mayotte, has come to Germany to gather information for a historical study on Burundi, the President of the island republic. She has a German father, and is fluent in the language. She hopes to get this information from Karlsbeck, a retired secret agent, who had been Burundi's advisor. Her real objective is to find incriminating material that could be used to sabotage Burundi's re-election

She works for the outlawed socialist opposition party lead by Uluguru. During the last election campaign Uluguru's predecessor Malim had blown up a power dam, a major development project, and had committed suicide. But there was circumstantial evidence that suggested that Burundi himself might have ordered the explosion and the murder of his political opponent. Diana fails to discover sufficient proof to discredit Burundi. Instead, she finds out that Karlsbeck had committed the murder in his capacity as a secret agent in the service of Britain. Diana tries to poison Karlsbeck, but does not succeed.

Peter Schmidt mentions that the Mayotte of his novel is not identical with the historical Mayotte, rather it could stand for any other strategically important Third World country. Schmidt's view of the future is pessimistic. Diana who came to Germany to help achieve changes in her country, gradually becomes affected by Karlsbeck's nihilism. To him all ideologies are suspect and all attempts to create a peaceful and just society futile, as long as mankind is incapable of transforming its yearning for peace into an instinct. From that point of view Ululega's belief that the future will be an age of the Africans is rejected implicitly.

If nothing else, these Africa-related crime novels shed light on a continent that is little known in Germany. Authors are in general concerned about the future of Africa and question the benefits of foreign intervention. Moreover, authors emphasize that they have no prejudices and attempt to give an unbiased portrait of Africa.

By doing so they make an important contribution in the fight against racial prejudice, and add a new dimension to the West German crime novel.

# Works Cited

A. Fiction

Grän, Christine. *Weisse sterben selten in Samyana (Whites Seldom Die in Samyana)*. Reinbek: Rowohlt, 1986.

Huby, Felix. "Leibwache" ("Bodyguard"). *Jeder kann's gewesen sein (Anybody Could Have Done It)*. Gerlingen: Bleicher, 1988. 77-94.

Klugmann, Norbert, and Peter Mathews. *Flieg, Adler Kühn (Fly, Eagle Kühn)*. Reinbek: Rowohlt, 1985.

Kolarz, Henry. *Kalahari (Kalahari)*. 1979. Bergisch Gladbach: Lübbe, 1988.

———. *Die roten Elefanten (The Red Elephants*, 1981. Frankfurt am Main: Ullstein, 1985.

Loest, Erich. *Waffenkarussell (Weapons Roundabout)*. 1968. Frankfurt am Main: Fischer, 1986.

Porter, Harry. *Todestrip nach Afrika (Deathtrip to Africa)*. Kommissar X. Rastatt: PMS Roman—und Zeitschriftenverlag, 1987.

Schmidt, Peter. *Die Stunde des Geschichtenerzählers (The Hours of the Storyteller)*. Reinbek: Rowohlt, 1986.

Weinert-Wilton, Louis. *Der Teppich des Gràuens (Carpet of Horrors)*. 1929. München: Goldmann, 1984.

Wolff, Detlef. *Katenkamp in Kenia (Katenkamp in Kenya)*. Reinbek: Rowohlt, 1983.


B. Other Works

Oguntoye, Katharina, May Opitz, and Dagmar Schultz. "Rassismus, Sexismus und vorkoloniales Afrikabild in Deutschland." *Farbe bekennen: Afrodeutsche Frauen auf den Spuren ihrer Geschichte*. Berlin: Orlanda Frauenverlag, 1986. 17-84.

Paeffgen, Manfred. *Das Bild Schwarz-Afrikas in der öffentlichen Meinung der Bundesrepublik Deutschland 1949-1972*. München: Weltforum Verlag, 1976.

Ridley, Hugh. "Germany in the Mirror of its Colonial Literature." *German Life and Letters* 28 (1975): 375-386.

Sadji, Amadon Booker. *Das Bild des Negro-Afrikaners in der deutschen Kolonialliteratur (1884-1945). Ein Beitrag zur literarischen Imagologie*. Berlin: Dietrich Reimer, 1985.

# Chapter 7
# John Wyllie's West Africa:
# The Quarshie Novels

## Eugene P.A. Schleh

John Vectis Carew Wyllie (b. 1914) was born in India and later became a naturalized Canadian citizen. His varied career included four years in the British merchant marine, five years as an administrator for the British Red Cross, and positions in advertising, the film industry and television. A six year tour with the Royal Air Force included three years as a Japanese POW. In the 1950s he began to draw upon these experiences in his early novels. *The Goodly Seed* (1955) was a story of British and Dutch prisoners in a Japanese POW camp in Indonesia. Similarly, *Johnny Purple* (1956) was set in a 1942 British air base in Sumatra. In *Riot* (1957) Wyllie turned to his West African Red Cross years and wrote of the continent's simmering politics. After a lapse of some years he began a memorable series of mysteries set in the fictional country of Akhana (read Ghana) and featuring the exploits of an African physician, Dr. Samuel Quarshie.

Akhana is a typical product of the Scramble for Africa, an English-speaking island surrounded by French-speaking neighbors. Boundary lines fall where they may. "In 1885, in Berlin, they had drawn lines on maps, in a room some three thousand miles away from the territories they were bent on acquiring, without establishing what the boundaries they drew on their pieces of paper did to the people inhabiting the area. Thus the frontiers they planned

Published in *Clues*, vol. 8, no. 1 (Spring/Summer 1987). Reprinted with permission.

cut through the middle of kingdoms, tribes, clans, family lands and even ancient townships..." Even Quarshie's home village of Aduafo is divided by a wall. On both sides of the wall the people's native language is Goshi, but on one side their second language is French, while on the other it is English (K, 6).*

Such divisions, added to the multiplicity of ethnic groups within the country, result in fascinating and impressive linguistic patterns. Quarshie himself is a Goshi speaker who is able to converse fluently in French, English (both standard and pidgin), Hausa and presumably some other languages. Mrs. Quarshie comes from the other side of Akhana. She is Mante and speaks neither Goshi nor French, but she complements Quarshie by being fluent in Madu, Gondo and Kwi in addition, of course, to English.

Politically, Akhana has an all-too-typical West African history. Presumably Great Britain left the country with a democratically-elected leader. Whether he changed or was replaced we are not told, but the first ruler mentioned was a dictator, Prestor John, removed from the scene when he was shot by his secretary. Whether immediately or not, Prestor John was succeeded by President Aku Ompofolo whose assassination with a bomb is the subject of Quarshie's first case. At some later time, the military take over from a corrupt President, and Quarshie is recruited for cases by Head of State Colonel Jedawi or the very British, Sandhurst-educated Minister of Internal Affairs, Major Obruensi (J, 133).

The physical setting of Akhana is a striking blend of ultra modern and traditional. In Port St. Mary one can even find the Hexagon (with six sides to outdo the U.S.A.'s Pentagon) built by a former dictator to house the government ministries. Unfortunately there were not enough ministries to fill it, so the dictator had to create some new ones, Population Research and Aviation Planning (I, 52). Numerous "modern" apartments have been erected but their functionality is questionable. Mrs. Quarshie visits expatriate friends who are fortunate in having an old-style bungalow. Thus it is not dependent on air-conditioning like more recent buildings, which

---

*Text references are to pages in the novels listed by letter in the accompanying works cited.

are the hostages of the "unreliable generating equipment at the local power station" (A, 14).

At the same time life for most people is only marginally changed from pre-colonial times. The evening streets are described as a hubbub, with "crowds seething in every direction, the Muslim beggars, women of all sizes and ages carrying all kinds of things on their heads from sewing machines to baskets full of live chickens, the street vendors with little pyramids of kola nuts, kenke balls or canned milk in front of them as well as a hundred other items of merchandise..." (A, 133). Elsewhere a rural version of such a market is described and the merchandise further enumerated as "town imports" such as "soap, canned milk, Quaker Oats, sardines and cigarettes" which could be bought singly or in packets. Along side there were "local goods" such as cassava, yams, okra and green oranges, spices, pottery, and "strange looking goods" from herbalists and local fetish priests (I, 61).

Quarshie is not uncritical of some directions Westernization has taken. At one town he observes that while it still has a central market, now "instead of hand pumped gasoline from a cylinder atop a 60 gallon drum,...Esso, Caltex, Agip, BP and Shell filling stations displayed signs proclaiming their proprietary interests" (J, 12). At least twice he categorizes Western commercialism: "In dealing with the underdeveloped countries the main objective of the technologically proficient West has been to change a taste for good clean water into a taste for Coca-Cola" (J, 12; B, 60). He feels white men "have done their best to squash our traditional belief in community and have introduced us very forcibly to their charming world in which individualism and competition are corner-stones" (I, 127). At the same time Quarshie frequently enjoys his bottled beer and more significantly recognizes value, both physical and psychological, in some aspects of Westernization. Certainly he values his own education, and when Mrs. Quarshie questions the cost of building Akhana's own university, Quarshie makes clear it is important for people of a young nation to have something about which they can say: "Ours is better than theirs" (E, 63). She is critical of too much white influence and declares the white man "has invisible reins on us. He planted white brains in many of us. We have to think in his language, subscribe to his values, because he took all the others away" (I, 26). At another time it is Mrs. Quarshie, however, who points out to the Doctor that the journey they had just made in 12 hours would have taken 20 to 25 days before modern roads and transport (J, 12).

Dr. Samuel and Prudence Quarshie are skilled modern Africans who also retain links with and affection for traditional ways. They live in Port St. Mary, the capital city of Akhana, although their adventures take them to rural regions and even to neighboring countries.

Dr. Quarshie is close enough to his traditional roots to have tribal marks cut into his chest. His higher education as a physician was at McGill University, Montreal, Canada, and he is now Chief Medical Officer and Pathologist at the Port St. Mary City Infirmary. Mrs. Quarshie, before marriage, had been a Sister at the General Hospital in Port St. Mary and a tutor in midwifery. She continues to substitute for local nurse-midwives if needed and if the couple's crime-solving schedule permits.

Physically, the Doctor is a large, powerful man while Mrs. Quarshie is a short, plump beauty. Prudence, too, comes from a more traditional setting and had an alliteration-loving father who named his other daughters Patience, Probity, Piety, Perspicacity, Philanthropy and Pertinacity.

Quarshie is a cognitive detective capable of occasional violent action. His style is derived from his medical career. In his first case Quarshie describes how he handled difficult medical problems: "I go over every bit of information I have collected on the case, refreshing my mind on it and then I wait. When it works...and that is far from always...it is like electricity jumping across a gap and fusing together two separate elements. Quite often they are elements I would not have dreamed of putting together myself had I followed a methodical pattern of reasoning" (T, 8). Later his technique was described as "...he threw, metaphorically, all the facts, ideas and conclusions he had arrived at over his shoulder and then turned and faced them where they lay strewn behind him. It was a way of cleaning everything out of his system. Sometimes it led both to the discovery of something which had been lying concealed from sight under more recent concepts or information and to the bits and pieces falling into unexpected patterns" (F, 150-151).

At the same time Quarshie is capable of quick action and high violence. In one case he rescues Mrs. Quarshie by jumping and knocking out the villain (K, 169); in another his punch fractures the villain's jaw. His violence can go to extremes. In his last case to date Quarshie kills twice. First he dispatches an attacking secret policeman with a blow to the back of his neck, and then, lacking any faith in the neighboring country's police, he administers his own justice by delivering a lethal rabbit punch to the killer's neck (F, 131, 171).

The Quarshies have a small circle of family and friends who appear repeatedly throughout the series. The Doctor's uncle Ezra is the Permanent Secretary at the Ministry of Internal Affairs, and it is he who recruits Quarshie for his first case. In a later case Samuel and Prudence, childless themselves, adopt a twelve-year-old orphaned relative, Arimi, who later becomes a sometime assistant (K, 14). Finally there is their dearest friend, Jules, the gallant old French Ambassador, described as knowing "more about the history of West Africa than any other white man in the region" and helpful with both advice and contacts (E, 8).

Wyllie paints a complex, but accurate, picture of West Africa. It is a composite of Mercedes Benzes and fetish priests, of Western-university-educated professionals whose relatives may be animists who believe in the spiritual return of ancestors. It is an area that daily functions in two spheres, the Europeanized and the traditional, with the best of each not necessarily the rule. "Corruption was an accepted fact of life in Europeanized West Africa but usually only so long as it fell within reasonable limits and was not talked about" (A, 132). When it exceeds these limits, other Western innovations may appear, assassination and the coup.

The reader will gain other impressions from these novels. One is that expatriates, particularly black and white Americans, play an extraordinary role in the region's violent crime, both as victims and as perpetrators. In one case set in nearby Transniger, the case centers, in fact, on a plot to eliminate whites headed by a Chicago-born black American (B). In other cases expatriates kill or are killed while other expatriates appear in Quarshie's circle of friends, ranging from long-time residents, "old coasters," to more recent settlers and visiting academics. The white population of a nearby country, the Ebony Coast, is described as having risen from 5,000 at the time of independence to 50,000 (figures strongly suggestive of Ivory Coast in fact) (F, 20); from the numbers of Americans and Europeans Quarshie runs across, Akhana cannot be far behind.

Detecting can be exhausting, and the Quarshies develop a relaxing and most pleasant way to unwind after a taxing case. In a majority of the books they go home, the Doctor enjoys some beer, they talk a little about the case and then go to bed and make love. Outside rewards may be limited for this fascinating duo, but fortunately they can sustain themselves.

John Wyllie has made a significant contribution to the field of detective fiction. He has opened up a seldom-touched area of the world for Western readers and explored both traditional and Western values. In addition, he has given us all a delightful pair of sleuths. Prudence and Samuel Quarshie educate and entertain their readers. They have earned a lasting place in the world of literary detection.

# Works Cited

A   *The Butterfly Flood*. Garden City, NY: Doubleday and Company, Inc. (Published for The Crime Club), 1975

B   *Death Is A Drum...Beating Forever*. Garden City, NY: Doubleday and Company, Inc. (Published for The Crime Club), 1977

C   *The Goodly Seed*. New York: E.P. Dutton and Co., Inc. 1955.

D   *Johnny Purple*. New York: E.P. Dutton and Co., Inc., 1956.

E   *The Killer Breath*. Garden City, NY: Doubleday and Company, Inc. (Published for The Crime Club), 1979.

F   *The Long Dark Night of Baron Samedi*. Garden City, NY: Doubleday and Company, Inc. (Published for The Crime Club), 1981.

G   *A Pocket Full of Dead*. Garden City, NY: Doubleday and Company, Inc. (Published for The Crime Club), 1978.

H   *Riot*. New York: E.P. Dutton and Company., Inc., 1957.

I   *Skull Still Bone*. Garden City, NY: Doubleday and Company, Inc. (Published for The Crime Club), 1975.

J   *A Tiger in Red Weather*. Garden City, NY: Doubleday and Company, Inc. (Published for The Crime Club), 1980.

K   *To Catch A Viper*. Garden City, NY: Doubleday and Company, Inc. (Published for The Crime Club), 1977.

# Chapter 8
# Decolonization and Detective Fiction: Ngugi wa Thiong'o's *Petals of Blood*

## Steven R. Carter

Ernst Kaemmel, an East German critic, has argued, on somewhat questionable but thought-provoking grounds, that "the detective novel is a child of capitalism" (Kaemmel 1983: 57). Among other reasons, he insists that it upholds the sanctity of private property and romantically glorifies the activities of isolated individuals, and he further notes that "it arose in the most highly developed countries of premonopolistic capitalism, in England and the United States in the second half of the nineteenth century and the beginning of the twentieth" (p.57). This was also the period of the rise of colonization of Africa which may, perhaps more legitimately, be considered capitalism's child. Without accepting Kaemmel's contention that "with the latter's collapse" it "will likewise disappear" (p. 61), one may still observe some striking similarities in the literary images developed by capitalism's two supposed offspring, those of the classic detective and the colonial settler. Both detective and colonial fiction usually celebrate heroes who, while gloriously displaying their individuality and openly acknowledging their personal ambition and extraordinary self-confidence, bring order out of chaos or incoherent primitivism, retain their faith in logic and common sense in the face of the irrational and superstition, and defend the highest ideals of civilization. Moreover, two twentieth-century mysteries set in Kenya,

Published in *Clues*, vol. 8, no. 1 (Spring/Summer 1987). Reprinted in somewhat revised form with permission.

Elspeth Huxley's *Murder on Safari* and M.M. Kaye's *Death in Kenya*, even combine the two heroes into one figure and imply that the two value systems they represent are in reality only one. Huxley's Canadian-born colonial policeman, following Kaemmel's model, sets out to recover the stolen jewels of a wealthy woman by romantically individualistic investigative techniques. Kaye's settler-detective, Drew Stratton, not only uncovers the identity of a white land owner who has murdered fellow settlers but also blackens his body so that he can spy on the Mau Mau without any of them guessing he's an Englishman! He heartily approves of the killing and torturing of Africans by civilized men since "you cannot conduct a campaign against a bestial terror like the Mau Mau with gloves on" (Kaye 1983: 294). When Kaye's heroine timidly objects that "it *is* their country," Stratton self-righteously sets her straight:

> All the chatter about "It belongs to them"...makes me tired. Sixty years ago Americans were still fighting Red Indians and Mexicans and grabbing *their* land; but I've never heard anyone suggesting that they should get the hell out of it and give it back to the original owners. Our grandfathers found a howling wilderness that no one wanted, and which, at the time, no one objected to their taking possession of. And with blood, toil, tears and sweat they turned it into a flourishing concern. At which point a yelping chorus is raised, demanding, in the name of "Nationalism", that it be handed over to them. Well, if they are capable of running this on their own, or of turning a howling wilderness into a rich and prosperous concern, let 'em prove it! There's a hell of a lot of Africa. They can find a bit and start right in to show us. But that won't do for them. It's the fruit of somebody else's labour that they are after. (p. 295)

This speech is packed with an incredible number of distortions of Kenyan history and self-justifying lies about the imperialist land rip-off yet it clearly embodies both the detective and settler ideals of dedication, perseverance, individual achievement, respect for property that's been properly grabbed, and, of course, "fair play."

Granting that there are at least some significant connections between capitalism, colonialism and detective fiction, it becomes a question of considerable importance why Kenya's leading writer and radical, Ngugi wa Thiong'o, would choose to use the mystery form for a major attack on neo-colonialism. Lewis Nkosi, among other critics, has pointed out the need to pay closer attention to "a phenomenon common to the colonised: the adoption of models, whether linguistic or narrative structures, which have been bequeathed to them by the colonising master" (Nkosi 1981:18). Ngugi himself admits that in the writing of *Petals of Blood*, he "came to be more and more disillusioned with the use of foreign languages to express Kenya's soul or to express the social conditions of Kenya" (quoted in Killam 1980: 15). The question Ngugi raises about the adequacy of a foreign language to convey the values and spirit of a culture that is radically different from the one in which it was created applies to foreign narrative structures as well. Specifically, is it possible for an African writer to use a colonial language or narrative structure to make an effective anti-colonial statement or will the critical message be inevitably blunted by the medium in which it is expressed? Can African experience be honestly and fully portrayed in a European language or art form? Can even the most skilled African writer compel a colonial language or literary form to work against itself by exposing its underlying assumptions and countering them with a different set of assumptions? Above all, in this case, can the mystery form be manipulated and expanded into a fit vehicle for the de-mystification of "law" and "order" and "civilization" in a colonial or neo-colonial society?

Even though he may now feel "disillusioned" about the language and possibly the narrative structure he used in *Petals of Blood* and has switched to writing in Gikuyu and a more traditional African form, Ngugi clearly believed when he began writing it that all of these questions could be answered affirmatively. In his essay "Literature and Society," he argues that "most national liberation movements start by rejecting the culture of the colonizer, by repudiating the religion of the oppressing nation and class and the entire educational system of the colonizer. People create their own songs, poems, dances, literature, which embody a structure of values dialectically opposed to those of the ruling class of the oppressing race and nation. Often they will take the songs of the colonizer and give them an entirely different meaning, interpretation and emphasis" (Ngugi 1981: 27). The last sentence suggests Ngugi's own practice concerning western literary forms through *Petals of*

*Blood.* The chief example he cites of an oppressed people transforming the cultural products of their oppressor for their own purposes again implies Ngugi's former (and not entirely abandoned) approach to foreign literary forms and especially to detective fiction:

Mau Mau was Kenya's national liberation movement that opted for the armed struggle as the highest form of political and economic struggle. On top of demanding the land and power, they rejected the culture of the oppressor and created a popular oral literature embodying anti-exploitation values. They took Christian songs; they took even the Bible and gave these meanings and values in harmony with the aspirations of their struggle. Christians had often sung about heaven and angels, and a spiritual journey in a spiritual intangible universe where metaphysical disembodied evil and good were locked in perpetual spiritual warfare...The Mau Mau revolutionaries took up the same song and tune and turned it into a song of actual political, visible material freedom but here on earth, in Kenya (p. 27).

Just as the Mau Mau remade Christian songs into revolutionary ones, Ngugi turned the classic detective novel with its conservative social values into an anti-detective novel with a radical social vision. Through his construction and resolution of the mystery in *Petals of Blood*, Ngugi reveals and rejects most of the fundamental principles underlying classic detective fiction, including glorification of individual heroism and the effectiveness of individual effort, belief in the European social order and overwhelming value of civilization (meaning, of course, European civilization), idealization of the puzzle-solving intellect, and the conviction that facts have a high value in themselves divorced from their complex human context (a policeman's request to Munira to stick to facts echoes Sgt. Friday's well known, "Just give me the facts, ma'am," on *Dragnet*). Ngugi also repudiates such underpinnings of classic detective fiction as the belief in a system of ethics founded on either traditional western sources (including Protestantism, Catholicism, and English and American democratic ideals) or an individual code and the belief in the fixity of human nature. In contrast to the classic detective's attempt to determine which suspect has carefully concealed what he or she really is, Ngugi shows characters constantly changing and implies that "human nature" may be altered by altering the social structure.

A large part of Ngugi's three-pronged attack on capitalism, neo-colonialism and detective fiction is made through his portrayals of the murderer, Godfrey Munira, and the detective, Inspector Godfrey. As their sharing of the name "Godfrey" implies, the Inspector and Munira may, like Poe's Monsieur Dupin and Minister D in "The Purloined Letter," be mirror images of each other, though the mirror is a distorted one. There is not much of a distinction to be made between this criminal and this detective, unlike Ngugi's usually sharp distinction between the oppressed and the oppressor. But in a criminal system, what is a crime? Individual criminals must be viewed differently when the structure of society is the primary source of evil and viciousness.

Inspector Godfrey serves the state; his only interest in human beings is as components of a puzzle and he puts his puzzle solving abilities at the behest of whatever authority controls his state. His discovery that Munira set the fire that killed Chui and Mzigo solves none of the underlying social problems, and he even fails to discover that Wanja killed Kimeria with a panga after observing that her wood mansion was on fire. His limited "success" as a detective underlines his human failings in understanding his fellow human beings and his function in his society. His "heroism" thus is ultimately more harmful than beneficial; he is on the side of the oppressor rather than the oppressed. This becomes obvious through his readiness to regard the radical Karega as the chief suspect, even though he is the only one of the four suspects to have an alibi. And because Inspector Godfrey is so suspicious of him, we are too. As Cook and Okenimpke point out, "it is no part of Ngugi's scheme to have Karega exterminating the handful of individual oppressors whose deaths shape the plot—though at the level of a 'who-done-it?' detective story we are meant wrongly to suspect him, and at another level to find food for thought when we discover our mistake" (Cook 1983: 97).

Part (though by no means all) of the food for thought comes from our awareness of Inspector Godfrey's eagerness to torture Karega on the basis of so little evidence against him (and if we have shared his attitudes, we must share his guilt), his lack of remorse when he learns that Karega is innocent, and his equanimity concerning Karega's continued incarceration on the suspicion that he is a "communist at heart" (Ngugi 1977: 344). Because he regards "the system of private ownership, of means of production, exchange and distribution" as "synonymous with the natural order of things like the sun, the moon and the stars," he considers people like Karega who challenge that system as a threat to the "ordained fixity and permanence of things" and "as such they were worse than murderers" (p. 333). Belief in the social order is one of the standard values of the classic detective, but here it is exposed as a great social evil. Although Inspector Godfrey has never taken a bribe or acquired much property, he is proud to have helped protect a system enabling other men to become rich, and he reflects that "everybody, even those millionaires that had ganged together under Kamwene Cultural Organization, really owed their position to the force. The police force was truly the maker of modern Kenya, he had always felt" (p. 334). Given the hideous nature of the Kamwene Cultural Organization (KCO) which was formed strictly as a means of forcing the Gikuyu poor by trickery and brutality to support the rich members of their ethnic group, this is a devastating admission.

Even though he has no second thoughts about what he has done to the innocent man, Karega, the Inspector feels more sympathy and respect for the guilty one, Munira, and this leads him temporarily to call into question some of his most basic positions. He is equally amazed that Munira could turn his back on "his father's immense property" and that he "was prepared to murder in the name of moral purity" (p. 334). Munira's concern for moral purity prompts the Inspector to consider that "this system of capitalism and capitalistic democracy needed moral purity if it was going to survive" and that perhaps he should do something about "the skeletons that he himself had come across in the New Ilmorog" (p. 334). He had not been much interested in "moral purity" before, having carefully restricted himself to the puzzles that were presented to him and feeling that larger social issues were not part of his job. However, he now begins to wonder if he should expose the "smuggling of gemstones and ivory plus animal and even human skins" that went on under the cover of the Utamaduni Cultural Tourist Center set up by the MP Nderi wa Riera. A short time earlier, Munira had joked with him that the only difference between the black market smugglers in WWII and the present day smugglers of "ivory and rubies, maize and charcoal" is that the current ones would never be chased by policemen (p. 330). Inspector Godfrey now proves the truth of Munira's assertion by deciding to officially overlook the smuggling at the Tourist Center because there are too many VIP's involved. Instead, "he would keep the report and the knowledge to himself" since "it might come in useful should he ever be called upon to put together another criminal jigsaw puzzle" (p. 335). By making this decision, the Inspector reveals that his attitude toward puzzle-solving is really a cop-out, a rationalization that enables him to condone corruption as long as it isn't directly related to any of his cases. This attitude is closely akin to that of most classic detectives and novelists. Note, for example, Julian Symons's praise of S.S. Van Dine for his "disdainful disregard of everything except the detective and the puzzle" and his argument that this quality coupled with Van Dine's "outrageous cleverness" place his work "among the finest fruits of the Golden Age" of detective fiction (Symons 1972: 113). Thus, Ngugi's attack on Inspector Godfrey's amoral retreat into puzzles hits directly at the base of classic detective fiction—and shatters it. Ngugi goes even further, however; his view, carefully developed throughout the novel, is that even if everyone in the capitalist system should miraculously become morally pure overnight that would not be enough to make the system just since it is founded on oppression and this oppression would remain. Chasing Muniras is among the greatest of cop-outs if only because it affords a way of avoiding the most urgently needed action for achieving true justice, namely the struggle to change the social order.

Like Inspector Godfrey's image of himself as a puzzle-solver, Godfrey Munira's image of himself as a spectator or outsider protects him from having to take a stand against the evils around him as well as from facing the consequences of his actions. Worse still, when he finally decides to make a heroic effort to cast off the role of spectator and become a man of action, he, like the Inspector, chooses the wrong target and equally fails to come to terms with the true social problems. His killing of three oppressors (two directly, one indirectly) is accidental; his target for murder was Wanja, a victim whom he, with the typically Christian puritanical distorted view of sexuality, had mistaken for chief villain, even the devil.

Another major way in which Munira resembles Inspector Godfrey is that he has absorbed—and been warped by—European establishment values without being fully aware of this. His name Munira, which in Gikuyu means "stump," recalls one of the most striking stanzas in Okot p'Bitek's *Song of Lawino*, a poem which Ngugi discussed in his essay collection *Homecoming*, and which is one of the pitifully few books that Munira owns. In this poem Lawino, a village woman, laments the effects of a western university education on her husband Ocol, arguing:

> And the reading
> Has killed my man.
> In the ways of his people
> He has become
> A stump. (quoted in Gurr 1981: 98)

Munira, as much a stump in this sense as Ocol, shows just how little he knows about the ways of his people during the communal singing on the eve of the circumcision rites when he tries "a verse he thought he knew" and fails to complete it, prompting Njuguna and Nyakinua to chide:

> You now break harmony of voices
> You now break harmony of voices
> It's the way you'll surely break out harmony
> When the time of initiation comes. (Ngugi 1977: 209)

Njuguna's and Nyakinyua's ironically appropriate warning that Munira would break the harmony also during the rites of initiation into manhood and womanhood implies that Munira has not fully achieved manhood and experiences problems concerning his sexuality. Munira partially confirms this by confessing to Abdullah "how he had always felt a little incomplete because he had been circumcised in hospital under a pain killer, so that he never really felt that he truly belonged to his age-group: Gicina Bangi" (p. 204). In this respect, too, Munira may be compared to

Ocol in *Song of Lawino* since, according to Andrew Gurr, Lawino equates Ocol's "withdrawal from the ways of his people with castration. Educated youths are lifeless stumps.

> Their manhood was finished
> In the classroom
> Their testicles
> Were smashed
> With large books! (Gurr 1981: 98)

Even though there is no hint that Munira is impotent or physically a eunuch (and neither is Ocol), all of his sexual relationships are troubled and most of his problems with them can be traced to Christianity and Christian-oriented education. His first sexual experience is with a prostitute named Amina and afterwards he returns home with "a consciousness of the enormity of the sin he had earlier committed" (Ngugi 1977: 14). This consciousness of having done wrong, according to the Christian standards his father (an elder in the Presbyterian Church) had drilled into him, is so great that he builds "an imitation of Amina's house at Kamiritho where he had sinned against the Lord, and burnt it" (p. 14). This, of course, foreshadows or, in detective fiction terms, provides a clue to his later attempt to burn Wanja's house—and Wanja—for similar motives. However, looked at more closely, this incident reveals that Munira experienced shame as well as guilt. As Munira later reflects:

She had really humiliated him. "He is only a boy," she said..."You know I don't sleep with uncircumcised men. It's a rule of mine. But come here."...Munira was trembling with fear and shame and he wanted to cry. But she was nice and she had soothed him with the gentleness of a mother and now he felt he would die if—But she had put him between her fleshy thighs...crossed her legs slightly and, God, it was all over for him and he could not tell if he had been in or not. It was this that he had tried to exorcise by fire in vain. (pp. 71-72)

Munira's second recounted sexual experience also includes references to both circumcision and Christianity in a way that suggests that they involve opposing sets of values and lead to vastly different experiences. (The opposition of Christians in Kenya to circumcision as a pagan ritual was a major theme in Ngugi's first written novel, *The River Between*). Evidently Munira's Christian father had opposed circumcision since "as a boy Munira used to hide from home to listen to the singing which accompanied the ceremony" (p. 203). Significantly, "it was during one of the ceremonies that he had met Julia his future wife. She was then Wanjiru. Her voice, her dancing, her total involvement had attracted him and he had decided that here at last was what would bring fulfillment to his life. But she had become Julia and the temporary dream of an escape into sensuality had vanished on the marriage bed" (p. 203). After Wanjiru converted to Christianity and changed her name to Julia, "too much righteous living and Bible-reading and daily prayers had drained her of all sensuality and what remained now was the cold incandescence of the spirit" (p. 16).

Following the loss of his dream of sensual fulfillment with Wanjiru, Munira seems to recover the dream with Wanja and the first time they make love seems to be the only fully satisfying sexual experience in his life. It is so satisfying, in fact, that it becomes the basis for his obsession with Wanja. However, even this experience eventually becomes a source of humiliation to him when Wanja informs him that she had been following the diviner Mwathi wa Mugo's instructions that night in the hope of becoming pregnant. His pained reaction to this, "so she was only using him, for a witchdoctor's experiment?," reveals not only his awareness of another failure in his life but also his Christian-induced contempt for pagan religions since no tradition-respecting African would have called Mwathi a "witchdoctor" (p. 250). Once again, he shows how far removed from his roots he is, suffering as much shame over having been touched by paganism as over having been manipulated. Later, when she humiliates him further by choosing Karega over him, Munira responds by getting Karega fired from the subordinate teaching job that he, Munira, had originally given him. At this point, the unnamed narrator tells us something about Munira's motivation for this action that neither Munira nor Karega understands. After observing that Karega "was ignorant of Munira's attachment to Wanja," the narrator continues:

And even if he had known, he would not have understood. He was too young. He was innocent. He did not as yet know of those doubts that needed affirmations of passion to silence them and which, unsilenced, could drive the middle-aged to murder even as an act of self-affirmation and assurance that one had not really failed. Had Lord Freeze-Kilby not followed his goodly lady with gun and powder originally meant for natives and animals? So Karega could only see motiveless paltriness in Munira's act of vengeance. (pp. 252-253)

Here is another clue pointing to Munira's future attempt to murder Wanja, but what is even more significant is that Munira's doubts about his sexuality, his jealousy, his distress at being middle-aged and his capacity to murder for all three motives parallel the forces that drove Lord Freeze-Kilby to murder his wife, a parallel that suggests that perhaps these forces have their origin in European attitudes and may be acquired from a western education. In spite of these pressures, however, Munira manages to maintain some measure of control until Wanja, in a long delayed vengeance for his driving Karega away from her, humiliates Munira one last time by making him become her first paying customer at her new brothel after leading him to believe she was interested in him again. Then Munira becomes converted to evangelical Christianity and starts to view Wanja as "carrying the power of satanic evil" and the stage is set for murder (p. 295). Ironically, Munira's reason for finally taking action against her is that he wants to save his former rival, Karega, from falling into her power because he now views Karega as almost a younger version of himself:

From nowhere, a voice spoke to him: She is Jezebel, Karega will never escape from her embrace of evil. In the dark, the message was clear: Karega had to be saved from her. He would otherwise descend the very same steps that Munira himself descended (p. 332).

The final irony, though, is that Munira, like Inspector Godfrey, finds his justification for an inhumane and vicious act in the belief that he is performing a duty to the law. However, whereas Inspector Godfrey is committed to man's law and the social order, Godfrey Munira is devoted to God's Law:

He was doing this only in active obedience to the Law. It was enjoined on him to burn down the whorehouse—which mocked God's work on earth. He poured petrol on all the doors and lit it up...He, Munira, had willed and acted, and he felt, as he knelt down to pray, that he was no longer an outsider, for he had finally affirmed his oneness with the Law. (pp. 332-333)

All the details about Munira's sexual problems would have been enough to satisfy two types of mystery. For classic detective fiction, they provide clues to identify Munira as the one who set fire to Wanja's mansion. For the psychological crime novel, they help develop a fascinating case history. However, Ngugi demonstrates the inadequacy of both approaches by placing Munira's thoughts and behavior in a larger context. Ngugi's focus is on the ways in which western civilization, and particularly Christianity, has distorted and perverted sexuality. Other examples of sexuality distorted and perverted by western civilization abound: the West German's attempt to induce Wanja to have sex with a dog, Cambridge Fraudsham's unnatural attachment to his dog after having been betrayed by a woman, the hymn loving Lillian's need to pretend to be a virgin every time she goes to bed with a man, the smutty mockery of the circumcision ceremony by Chui's westernized guests, and the aging European tourists' desire for young African virgins to deflower (giving a more sinister twist to the title *Petals of Blood* and suggesting the basic European intent toward Africa). Moreover, in addition to turning people into emotional cripples, this heavy and unhealthy emphasis on sex directs attention away from economic, social and political evils of colonialism and neo-colonialism. As Ime Ikiddeh has pointed out, Ngugi views colonialism and capitalism "as twin brothers whose mission is to exploit the material wealth of subject peoples, and who, in order to gain acceptability and perpetuation, enlist the services of their more sly but attractive first cousins, Christianity and Christian-oriented education, whose duty is to capture the soul and the mind as well" (forward to Ngugi 1972: xii). One important way Christianity operates to capture the minds of the colonized and others is by getting them to focus on their own individual sins, particularly sexual sins, and the sexual sins of others rather than on the evil inherent in their social structure which enables some people to live off others and what can be done about this. Instead of killing Kimeria, Chui and Mzigo by accident, Munira should have been trying to kill them on purpose; after all, the three of them together stole his slogan "Theng'a Theng'a with Theng'eta" and reaped large profits from this publicity, Chui led Munira into a revolt for which he was not truly prepared and which cost him his place at school, Mzigo refused to give him any help in building up a school at Ilmorog but took credit for his achievement (not to mention their worse crimes against Munira's friends). However, Munira takes out his frustration not on them but on another of their victims because, in part, Christianity has led him to view her sexuality as an evil far greater than that of exploitation of the people. Similarly, when Munira's father learns that his son has committed murder, he considers himself partly to blame, not because of his greed or his role in helping to maintain a repressive power structure but because of "his sin of attempted adultery" with Karega's mother (p. 342). For healthy sex to flourish, a healthy society is needed, and this clearly means a society free from Christianity, capitalism and any form of exploitative relationship.

Eustace Palmer claims that "Munira's transformation into a religious fanatic at the end is one of the novel's major weaknesses. A violent death seems to be a logical and well-deserved conclusion to the fortunes of the three African directors of the Theng'eta Brewery, but that it should be brought about by a fire started in a moment of inspiration by a religious fanatic seems a melodramatic contrivance which takes a remarkably serious work back to the level of the detective thriller" (Palmer 1979:297). In taking this position, Palmer overlooks or distorts several important points. First, he makes the usual false distinction between "serious work" and "detective thriller" instead of the true distinction between serious detective fiction, such as works by John le Carré, Dashiell Hammett, Ross Macdonald and Umberto Eco, and either less serious or less successful detective fiction, such as works by Mickey Spillane, Richard Prather, Agatha Christie, etc. Second, he passes over the careful preparation of Munira's conversion to evangelical Christianity, thus providing a major foreshadowing of his conversion. Then, after his humiliation at the tea-drinking party (the oath-taking), we see him re-evaluating his Christian father and starting to admire his strength in standing up for the Christian faith. This is the result of Munira's perception of his own weakness and his wish that he could have stood up for his beliefs. He begins to see Christianity at this time as a refuge from the shame of his experience with the KCO and even his father's revelation that he took this oath voluntarily and expects to see a church branch of the KCO develop soon fail to turn Munira completely away from this new attraction to the church. When his respect for his father is undercut again by the revelation of the dictatorial way he treated Munira's sister and his responsibility for her suicide, Munira can no longer find refuge from alienation and humiliation in either his father or his father's church. However, Lillian offers him the option of a different form of Christianity which would enable him to submerge his weakness in God's strength and his alienation in communal fanaticism; it is the escape he has been seeking all his life. Third, and most important, Palmer misses the deliberate irony in the deaths of these men not being directly related to their villainy, the way in which Ngugi consciously plays upon our expectations, based on the conventional detective thriller, to surprise us into an awareness of the ultimate irrelevance of both the murders and their investigation to the major problems facing modern Kenya. Karega's explanation to Inspector Godfrey about why he would not have considered murdering these three exploiters helps to underlines this point:

I don't believe in the elimination of individuals. There are many Kimerias and Chuis in the country. They are the products of a system, just as the workers are products of a system. It's the system that needs to be changed...and only the workers of Kenya and the peasants can do that. (Ngugi 1977: 308)

As this passage implies, *Petals of Blood* categorically rejects every solution to the problems of modern Kenya (and capitalistic societies in general) that falls short of complete alteration of the social structure. As we have already seen, the first and foremost solution to be rejected is that of individual heroism. Even the radical organizer Karega, who often voices Ngugi's ideas, is not a hero in the traditional sense. He knows that he can't accomplish much by himself. He is still in jail at the end and has to depend on his fellow workers to demonstrate to get him out and the last lines of the novel emphasize his sense of unity with them "and he knew he was no longer alone" (p. 345). The novel also rejects love as a solution to social problems. Two of the tenderest and most genuinely affectionate relationships in the book, those between Karega and Munira's sister Mukami and between Karega and Wanja, are broken up by persons in positions of power, Munira's father and Munira. Another hope demonstrated to be hollow is reliance on the objective intellect, the belief that a brilliant and dispassionate man like Sherlock Holmes could find a solution that would be fair to everybody. This hope is effectively undercut by the lawyer's advice to Karega:

Educators, men of letters, intellectuals: these are only voices—not neutral, disembodied voices—but belonging to bodies of persons, of groups, of interests. You, who will seek the truth about words emitted by a voice, look first for the body behind the voice. The voice merely rationalises the needs, whims, caprices, of its owner, the master. Better therefore to know the master in whose service the intellect is and you'll be able to properly evaluate the import and imagery of his utterances. You serve the people who struggle; or you serve those who rob the people. (p. 200)

This statement provides a scathing indictment of Inspector Godfrey, who claims to be objective but who serves the State, and Godfrey Munira, who places his intellect at the service of a form of Christianity that is funded by American capitalists. Karega, on the other hand, *serves* the oppressed; he does not singlehandedly set out to save them as if he were a superman. Among other projected solutions proven to be equally hollow are: religion (Karega observes that "religion, any religion was a weapon against the workers"— p. 305); reform (the activities of the lawyer, though well-intentioned and temporarily successful in a limited sense, bring only minor changes at most in his society); individual virtue; individual vice; individual revolt; and individual salvation (if Wanja's salvation takes on an importance beyond this, it is because she is seen more as a representative of the people than as an individual). The two solutions that gain Karega's—and Ngugi's—approval are the worker's movement, which shows its strength through large-scale, highly unified strikes and demonstrations, and neo-Mau Mau organizations like the "Wakombozi—or the society of one world liberation" which kill systematically through a co-ordinated mass effort to force social change. In Ngugi's eyes, anything less is doomed to failure. This heavy emphasis on the need for mass effort rather than individual action to accomplish anything significant runs counter not only to classic detective fiction but also to the hard-boiled private eye novel.

In addition to attacking virtually every premise underlying classic detective fiction, Ngugi also challenges its basic structure. By mixing a variety of forms—prose, poetry, song; myth, history, social realism; psychological case study, fantasy, melodrama; the mainstream novel, the popular novel, orature—Ngugi resoundingly repudiates the rigid, exclusionary format of classic detective fiction. This mixture of forms also helps to redefine the idea of "popular" in popular culture. As we have already seen, Ngugi has taken a form that is nominally popular, classic detective fiction, and revealed its underlying premises to be elitist and ultra-conservative. His counterview, obviously, has been that the truly popular work can only be one honestly representing the situation and aspirations of the peasants and workers and that the main goal of such popular literature should be to arouse people to strive to create a society that eliminates any distinction between individuals that permits one person to exploit another. His practice of blending supposedly "high" and "low" forms itself provides a powerful reinforcement of the goal of eliminating elitist distinctions.

In addition, this practice appears to mark an alignment with the view of form taken in much traditional African "orature" (a term, which Ngugi has helped to popularize, meaning "oral literature"). Ngugi has argued that a study of the Oral Tradition would be "important" not only "in rehabilitating our minds, but also in helping African writers to innovate and break away from the European literary mainstream" (Ngugi 1972: 16). As is so often the case with Ngugi, his artistic practice seems again to conform closely to his theory. Consider the description that he and two fellow teachers made of orature:

Another point to be observed is the interlinked nature of art forms in traditional practice. Verbal forms are not always distinct from dance, music, etc. For example, in music there is close correspondence between verbal and melodic tones; in "metrical lyrics" it has been observed that poetic text is inseparable from tune; and the "folk tale" often bears an "operatic" form, with sung refrain as an integral part. *The distinction between prose and poetry is absent or very fluid.* (Ngugi 1972: 147, emphasis added)

Ngugi's unusually extensive practice of including not only lengthy passages of poetry but also song lyrics in an essentially prose work and of rapidly shifting between prose and poetry certainly fits this description. Moreover, *Petals of Blood* has much in common with the mixture of forms in the Congo epic, especially the Mwindo epic which had been translated into English well before the time Ngugi started his novel and which Ngugi, as a teacher of orature, would surely have studied. Consider how closely *Petals of Blood* matches Daniel Biebyck's 1972 description of the Congo epic (bearing in mind that since Ngugi had not yet chosen to write in Gikuyu he would not have been restricted to seeking a Gikuyu oral form for a model):

The epic is, so to speak, a supergenre that encompasses and harmoniously fuses together practically all genres known in a particular culture. The Mwindo epic is typical in this respect. There are prose and poetry in the epic, the narrative being constantly intersected with songs in poetic form. The prose narrative to some extent, and the songs to a larger extent, incorporate proverbs, riddles, praises, succinct aphoristic abstracts of tales, prayers, improvisations, and allusions and references to "true" stories and persons. (quoted in Chinweizu 1983: 76-77)

In addition to the forms already mentioned, *Petals of Blood* includes several animal fables told by Abdulla, Nyakinua's oral retelling of the founding of Ilmorog by the former herdsman Ndemi, an account of the "epic journey" of the people of Ilmorog to the city (Ngugi 1977: 143 and 184), satire (as in the names of Cambridge Fraudsham, Lord Freeze-Kilby and Sir Swallow Bloodall), allusions to true stories and persons (including Dedan Kimathi and Jomo Kenyatta), and a large number of political speeches. Whatever its source of inspiration, Ngugi's work surely qualifies as a "supergenre" to the same extent as the Mwindo epic and to an extent that few western novels and no classic detective novels have reached.

While Ngugi may not have deliberately set out with the intention I have been suggesting of Africanizing the western form of classic detective fiction, he has beyond doubt introduced into the classic detective form an African content and a mixture of other forms (some of which are African) that have never been attached to it before and he has done so in a way that bears some resemblance to African orature. At the same time, he has remained true to the one absolutely essential requirement of classic detective fiction, to provide a mystery with a set of clues that permit the reader to have a fair chance to guess the solution. Even though these clues are not laid out and explained at the end by an arrogant detective who thereby dazzles the reader with his intellectual prowess, they are present and may be pieced together by any reader who is willing to take on the role of detective.

Ngugi's combination of forms indicates that his work belongs to a new form of detective fiction, the experimental mystery. The characteristics of the form, as I defined it in an article on "Ishmael Reed's Neo-Hoodoo Detection," are:'

1) it combines elements of detective and crime fiction with the devices of mainstream and/or experimental fiction; 2) it reshapes the elements of detective and crime fiction to fit a personal vision; 3) it usually examines the mysteries of the spirit and/or the skeletons in the closets of societies (it generally aims at exposing the spiritual weaknesses of entire societies rather than ferreting out the hidden villainy of a single individual; it is closer to metaphysics and sociology that to intellectual gamesmanship and psychology); 4) it may or may not resolve any puzzle or problem it poses; and 5) the detective and crime novel elements must play a major role in the work as a whole. (Carter 1976: 273-274)

In addition, the essence of the experimental mystery form is a fruitful clash between the artist's view of life and the previously established forms of detective fiction, as between the conservative values of classic detective fiction and Ngugi's socialist values.

Clearly *Petals of Blood* fits all of the characteristics of the experimental mystery in my definition and even goes beyond it by forcing a change in the first part of the definition to include orature alongside the mainstream and experimental novel. Like Ishmael Reed's *Mumbo Jumbo*, *Petals of Blood* goes much further back in time than the period of the individual crime that is the ostensible focus of the narrative to the origins of a society and the distortion of its structure that is the real crime in the author's eyes. The real "mystery" here is why post-independence Kenya failed to become truly independent and all the clues point to the capitalist structure and ties of the new black bourgoisie with western financiers and governments. In leading us to detect the source of evil here and see the appropriate means of action against it, Ngugi has remained true to his deepest values and has proven that his chosen form can contain them. Moreover, he has, in effect, liberated the mystery genre in two major ways: 1. by showing that it need not be inextricably linked to capitalist and colonial values and 2. by showing that it need not be tied to European culture. His harmonious blending of elements of African orature (animal fables, ritual songs, perhaps even epic structure) with elements of mainstream and detective fiction offers an immeasurable enrichment of the form and effective proof that it can be Africanized. Above all, Ngugi demonstrates that in the hands of a creative master with sufficient insight and skill any form, no matter how rigid in format and underlying premises, can be enlarged and modified to embody an antithetical vision so that politically committed writers may choose whatever form they want provided they are fully aware of its premises and their own goals.

This essay was written for a National Endowment for the Humanities Summer Seminar on African Fiction under the brilliant and sensitive direction of Dr. David Dorsey. While Dr. Dorsey disagreed with some parts of the essay, he was the inspiration for the best elements of it.

# Works Cited

Carter, Steven R. "Ishmael Reed's Neo-Hoodoo Detection," in *Dimensions of Detective Fiction*, ed. Larry N. Landrum, Pat Browne and Ray B. Browne 265-274. Bowling Green, Ohio: The Popular Press, 1976.

Chinweizu, Onwuchekwa Jemie and Ihechukwu Madubuike. *Toward the Decolonization of African Literature, Vol. I.* Washington, D.C.: Howard University Press, 1983.

Cook, David and Michael Okenimpke. *Ngugi was Thiong'o: An Exploration of His Writings.* London: Heinemann, 1983.

Gurr, Andrew. *Writers in Exile.* Sussex: The Harvester Press, 1981.

Kaemmel, Ernst. "Literature Under the Table: The Detective Novel and Its Social Mission," in *The Poetics of Murder: Detective Fiction and Literary Theory,* ed. Glenn W. Most and William W. Stowe, 55-61. New York: Harcourt Brace Jovanovich, 1983.

Thiong'o, Ngugi wa. *Homecoming: Essays on African and Caribbean Literature, Culture and Politics.* New York: Lawrence Hill, 1972.

_____ *Petals of Blood.* London: Heinemann, 1977.

_____ *Writers in Politics.* London: Heinemann, 1981.

Nkosi, Lewis. *Tasks and Masks: Themes and Styles of African Literature.* London: Longman, 1981.

Palmer, Eustace. *The Growth of the African Novel.* London: Heinemann, 1979.

Symons, Julian. *Mortal Consequences: A History from the Detective Story to the Crime Novel.* New York: Harper and Row, 1972.


*Additional Sources*

Killam, G.D. *An Introduction to the Writings of Ngugi.* London: Heinemann, 1980.

Robson, Clifford B. *Ngugi wa Thiong'o.* London: Macmillan, 1979.

# Chapter 9
# South Africa

**Eugene Schleh**

With its large European stock population, it is not surprising that the history of Detective/Mystery fiction in South Africa parallels that in Europe. There is a particular relationship with English literary trends, but Afrikaans language authors have fully adopted the mystery genre. In addition to home-grown authors, many European and American writers have chosen South Africa as a setting. This has been particularly true because of the plot possibilities to be found in the land of such vast quantities of diamonds and gold.

South Africa has always been a segregated society and this appeared in the setting of the novels. Since the institution of the apartheid policy by the National Party in 1948, the relations between whites and non-whites and between South Africa and much of the world, have become almost inescapable elements in all fiction set in the country. Separate African residential locations, job reservation by race, laws against mixed-marriage and inter-racial sexual relations and sanctions leveled against South Africa by other countries all feature prominently in mystery fiction. It has become almost unthinkable to set a novel in South Africa without dealing with race relations. One could follow the development of apartheid through fiction; one can only hope to be able to follow the dismantling of the system now that the government has decided to end it.

# South African Detective Stories
# From 1951-1971*
### Susan Friedland

1. Airth, Rennie. *Snatch.* London, Cape, 1969. 248 p. Geneva.
2. Bennett, Jack. *Ocean road.* London, Joseph, 1967. 208 p. Dar es Salaam.
3. Black, Lionel. *Chance to die.* London, Cassell, 1965. 185 p. Swaziland-murder.
4. Brechin, David. *Nic Barber I.D.B.* Cape Town, Nasionale boekhandel, 1963. 137 p. Johannesburg-illicit diamond buying.
5. Brechin, David. *Uncut Diamonds.* Cape Town, Nasionale boekhandel, 1969. 163 p. South Africa.
6. Butler, K.R. *A fall of rock.* London, Bles, 1967. 224 p. Rhodesia-murder.
7. Chase, James Hadley. *The vulture is a patient bird.* London, Hale, 1969. 190 p. Drakensburg range and Lesotho.
8. Clarke, Anna. *A mind to murder.* London, Chatto and Windus, 1971. 200 p. London.
9. Cleeve, Brian Talbot. *Dark blood, dark terror.* London, Hammond, 1966. 251 p. Johannesburg, London, Zurich and the Congo.
10. Cleeve, Brian Talbot. *Portrait of my city.* London, Jarrold, 1952. 208 p. Johannesburg.
11. Creasey, John. *Call the Toff.* London, Hodder and Stoughton, 1953. 192 p. Cape Town and Johannesburg.
12. Creasey, John. *Gideon's sport,* by J.J. Marric [pseud]. London, Hodder & Stoughton, 1970. 192 p. (King crime) London.

*Extracts from *South African Stories in English and Afrikaans/From 1951-1971* a bibliography compiled by Susan Friedland. Johannesburg: University of the Witwatersrand, Department of Bibliography, Librarianship and Typography, 1972. Note that in addition to the English language authors listed here, the bibliography lists 381 Afrikaans language books. Reprinted with permission.

13. Creasey, John. *Murder, London-South Africa: a new story of Roger West of the yard.* London, Hodder and Stoughton, 1966. 190 p. South Africa-diamond smuggling.

14. Creasey, John. *A promise of diamonds: a crime haters story,* by Gordon Ashe [pseud.]. London, Long, 1965. 184 p. London and the Kalahari desert.

15. Croudace, Glynn. *Blackadder.* London, Macmillan, 1969. 190 p. South Africa-murder and diamond smuggling.

16. Croudace, Glynn. *Motives for murder.* South Africa, Central News agency, 1957. 175 p. (Dassie books) South Africa-murder.

17. Croudace, Glynn. *The scarlet bikini.* London, Macmillan, 1969. 157 p. Deep sea salvage operation on the coast of South West Africa-murder.

18. Desmond, Hugh. *The jacaranda murders.* London, Wright & Brown, 1951. 256 p. Durben.

19. Drin, Michael. *Signpost to fear.* Cape Town, Simondium, 1964. 189 p. Cape Town.

20. Driscoll, Peter. *The white lie assignment.* London, Macdonald, 1971. 211 p. London and the Mediterranean.

21. Drummond, June. *The black unicorn.* London, Gollancz, 1959. 224 p. Cape Town-murder.

22. Drummond, June. *Cable-car.* London, Gollancz, 1965. 190 p. Alpine valley of Champac.

23. Drummond, June. *Farewell party.* London, Gollancz, 1971. 191 p. Durban.

24. Drummond, June. *The Gantry episode.* London, Gollancz, 1968. 224 p. Gantry, a small town.

25. Drummond, June. *The people in glass house.* London, Gollancz, 1969. 192 p. London, New York and Amsterdam.

26. Drummond, June. *Welcome, proud lady.* London, Gollancz, 1964. 221 p. Cape-murder.

27. Du Camp, Alwyn. *Twana.* Clairwood, Mercantile printing works, printer, [1969?]. 207 p. South Africa.

28. Eland, Charles. *The desperate search.* London, Hale, 1971. 192 p. South Africa.

29. Farrington, Joseph. *The hand.* London, Jenkins, 1961. 176 p. Kenya.

30. Fearon, Diana. *Nairobi nightcap: a detective story*. London, Hale, 1958. 192 p. Nairobi.

31. Godfrey, Peter. *Death under the table*. Cape Town, S.A. scientific publishing co., 1954. 196 p. Cape Town.

32. Gray, Dulcie. *Baby Face*. London, Barker, 1959. 206 p. South Africa.

33. Harman, Neal. *Yours truly Angus MacIvor*. London, Barker, 1952. 237 p. Johannesburg.

34. Harris, Peter. *Cry hold*. London, Long, 1970. 184 p. Cape Town and the Karoo.

35. Harris, Peter. *The final set*. London, Long, 1965. 184 p. South Africa.

36. Harris, Peter. *Letters of discredit*. London, Long, 1964. 184 p. Cape Town.

37. Harris, Rex. *A hand in diamonds*. London, Constable, 1961. 247 p. South West Africa.

38. Huxley,*Mrs.* Elspeth Josceline. *The merry hippo: a novel*. London, Chatto and Windus, 1963. 254 p. Hapana-an imaginary African state.

39. Johns, Richard. *Man with a background of flames*. London, Dobson, 1954. 179 p. London.

40. Justin, Derek. *Shark's rock*. London, Elek, 1966. 159 p. South Africa.

41. Kaye, M.M. *Later than you think*. London, Longmans, 1958. 275 p. Kenya.

42. Knight, Frank. *Captains of the Calabar*. London, Lock. 1961. 183 p. Atlantic ocean, between West Africa and South Africa.

43. McClure, James. *The steam pig*. London, Gollancz, 1971. 224 p. South African town-Trekkesburg.

44. MacKenzie, Nigel. *Strange happening*. London, Wright and Brown, 1967. 173 p. Cape Town.

45. MacKinnon, Clark. *The flame lily*. London, Dakers, 1954. 228 p. Southern Rhodesia.

46. MacKinnon, Clark. *Leopard valley*. London, Long, 1963. 174 p. Rhodesia and the Transvaal.

47. MacKinnon, Clark. *Lost hyena*. London, Long, 1962. 184 p. Rhodesia.

48. Milne, Shirley. *False witness*. London, Hale, 1964. 189 p. South Africa.
49. Milne, Shirley. *The hammer of justice*. London, Hale, 1963. 191 p. Lesotho.
50. Milne, Shirley. *Stiff silk*. London, Hale, 1962. 192 p. Durban.
51. Monig, Christopher *pseud. Once upon a crime*. London, Boardman, 1960. 192 p. (American bloodhound, No. 290) Johannesburg.
52. Moodie, Edwin. *The great shakes*. London, Museum, press, 1956. 220 p. Johannesburg.
53. Moore, *Mrs.* Doris Langley. *All done by kindness: a novel*. London, Cassell, 1951. 315 p. Crime story.
54. O'Keefe, Bob. *Diamonds can be dangerous*. Pretoria, Spearhead publications, 1953. 190 p. Johannesburg-illicit diamond buying.
55. O'Keefe, Bob. *Gold without glitter*. South Africa, Central news agency, 1957. 166 p. (Dassie books) Barberton.
56. Paul, Ernest. *The Komespi affair*. London, Hale, 1968. 192 p. Europe and Cape Town.
57. Penrose, Margaret. *The fatal fifth*. London, Long, 1963. 183 p. Cape Town-murder.
58. Radford, Edwin. *Murder magnified: a doctor Manson detective novel*, by E. Radford and M.A. Radford. London, Hale, 1965. 190 p. South Africa.
59. Radford, M.A. *Murder magnified: a doctor Manson detective novel*, by E. Radford and M.A. Radford. London, Hale, 1965. 190 p. South Africa.
60. Scobie, Alastair. *The Cape Town affair*. London, Cassel, 1952. 215 p. Cape Town.
61. Seuffert, Muir. *Trespassers will die*. London, Hale, 1968. 192 p. Johannesburg.
62. Severn, Richard. *Stalk a long shadow*. London, Hale, 1967. 208 p. Johannesburg-diamond smuggling.
63. Stewart, Flora. *Blood relations*. London, Jenkins, 1967. 176 p. London.
64. Stewart, Flora. *Deadly nightcap*. London, Jenkins, 1966. 174 p. England-murder.

65. Van Rensburg, *Mrs.* Helen. *Death in a dark pool*, by Helen van Rensburg and Louwrens van Rensburg. London, Joseph, 1954. 239 p. Swaziland.

66. Van Rensburg, Louwrens. *Death in a dark pool*, by Helen van Rensburg and Louwrens van Rensburg. London, Joseph, 1954. 239 p. Swaziland.

67. Van Rensburg, *Mrs.* Helen. *The man with two ties*, by Helen van Rensburg and Louwrens van Rensburg. London, Joseph, 1955. 238 p. South Africa.

68. Wilson, David. *Murder in Mozambique.* London, Jenkins, 1963. 221 p. Mozambique.

69. York, Jeremy. *Safari with fear.* London, Melrose, 1953. 192 p. South Africa.

# Chapter 10
# Exploring the Mind of Evil:
# Wessel Ebersohn's Crime Fiction

### Fred Isaac

## I. Introduction

The mystery novel has become the major fictional form for the exploration of the constant war between forces which claim to be "Good" and "Evil". Frequently the protagonist and his enemy are less demonstrably black and white in monumental terms than there is an Evil individual, but this person may hide his or her inclinations behind mundane acts. Both readers and writers consider Murder, for example, as an ultimate Bad act, to be paid for by the killer by his life or at least his freedom.

The critical literature, too, has seldom investigated the differences between wrong, bad and Evil. There may be a sense that crime and the search for the criminal are sufficient for readers, that we are insufficiently interested in the moral aspects to care about or investigate the moral questions involved. This is of additional curiosity because there has never been any lack of interest in the idea of the hero as emblematic of the Right, the True, and the ultimate Good.

The battle which ensues between such forces would be inherently unequal, even if we did not know that the hero is destined to win. A sense of weakness at the core of the not-good as it is typically portrayed (in the guise of fury, vindictiveness or covetousness over primarily petty objects), conveys a false picture of the world and the people in it. In the context of the constant wars being waged between Detectives and villains, the subtext of

Good and Evil too frequently comes through as a bland and predictable skirmish.

The work of Wessel Ebersohn, however, points toward a discussion of serious moral questions and a clear comprehension by the reader of the true nature of Evil. In each of them he has presented a man whose intent is to change the world to fit his view. A reader coming to these books looking for dispassionate or controlled discussions will be sadly mistaken. Ebersohn's people are intent, they are dramatic, and above all, they are committed.

## II. Plots

Ebersohn has published 5 books since 1979. Two of them because they are not directly crime related, may be discussed quickly. *Store Up the Anger* (U.S. publication 1981) is a fictionalized biography of Steven Biko, the young black whose death as a result of South African police torture in 1977 became an international cause célèbre. The novel is a series of snapshots taken through the mind of the hero as he slips into and out of consciousness. In the present he notices the mundane under-furnished room he is in, while around him the bland and apathetic Security forces methodically attempt to break him. The rest of the time we learn about his early life in the townships and the various indignities which led him to become a militant, and ultimately a hunted enemy of the government of South Africa.

Most recently Ebersohn has published *Klara's Visitors* (Hamish Hamilton, 1987), an attempt to explore the early life of Adolf Hitler through his (fictitious) diaries. They take the reader through the Führer's life from earliest childhood to late 1931, showing his constant manic swings of behavior and attitude toward others. The other major character is a woman who represents Ebersohn's Freudian interpretation of Hitler's life. She appears as a servant in the family, the first prostitute he sees while in the army in World War I, and other passing figures. Her role is to excite Hitler sexually, but without allowing him release.

While the book is horrific in its image of Hitler, it compels the reader by its development of Hitler's psychosexual schizophrenia. We watch in awed fascination as he tries frantically to seduce his young niece but is unable to achieve erection. At the same time he controls his followers by a consuming sexual urge which transforms him into a state approaching amnesia and brings out the bestial voice that we know from the Newsreels and radio broadcasts of the 1930s. Even if questionable from a professional point of view, the combination may be as emotionally true a depiction of the Fuhrer's public persona as has appeared in fiction anywhere.

Ebersohn has not always been able to raise this level of passion, however. His first book, *The Centurion*, attempted to blend cyber-fiction with political drama. Published in 1979 by Johannesburg's Ravan Press, (and never released in either Great Britain or the U.S.) it tells of Dr. Gerald King, an experimental psychologist and writer. While attending a conference in Cairo, King is at the scene of a death-squad assassination intended to destroy the fragile Egyptian-Israeli peace just as true progress is possible. Examining one of the bodies of the attackers, he finds a battery near the young man's heart and an electrode connected to the base of his skull. Several hours later, when asked by the police to identify a body, King refuses when the wires he had earlier found do not appear in the second corpse. He publicly accuses the police of switching bodies, as much to verify his original visual memory as to call them liars.

On his return to England he recants under pressure from government agents. Later, however, he learns that his Egyptian interpreter died mysteriously within hours of King's departure for home. Gerald visits a friend, a wonderfully eccentric scientist named William Marshall who both confirms the death of the Egyptian and supports King's story. The two men then develop a list of scientists whose knowledge of the anatomy of the brain would allow them to work on an experiment such as he had seen. On returning home, though, King gets a further shock: one of the monkeys he has been using in an experiment has been murdered in a most brutal and meaningful way.

The following day Gerald travels to Scotland, where he finds that the great surgeon he wants to see has disappeared and is presumed dead. He visits the place along the Firth and confirms his suspicions about the "accident," but on his way back to his hotel is run over by a truck. Waking in the hospital the next day he finds that the enemies he senses have struck once more. The only photograph he has salvaged from Cairo has been stolen from his wallet. Later he is told by the police that the body of the lorry driver has been stolen from the morgue. Scotland Yard also turns against him when, on returning to London, he is met at the airport and his sole supporter on the Edinborough Police is suspiciously given a month's holiday. Finally, when he calls his friend in Cambridge, Marshall warns him off saying in a pained voice filled with unaccustomed fear "I am afraid, Gerald."

Increasingly terrified and puzzled, King goes to Cambridge, but is turned away by Marshall's previously timid wife. She accuses Gerald of causing the stroke her husband suffered after their telephone conversation. While staying underground with his lab assistant (the novel's love interest), he learns of Marshall's death and vows to uncover the source of the evil. Because he has heard of some research in South Africa that ties several missing brain researchers to the mysterious killings in Cairo, he decides to face the monster and flies down.

Arriving there, he discovers the apparent source of the evil, a newly opened but heavily guarded clinic outside Johannesburg. All of the eminent physicians whom he has sought are there, and he learns that they all have undergone "the operation," linking their brains to some sort of computerized controlling device. Their leader, called "The Chairman," is the Centurion of the title, leader of a hundred programmed monsters masquerading as the eminent men of science they once were. Through it all he is hunted by the minions of the experimenter, and he is finally captured. A short concluding scene leaves the reader wondering about who the Centurion is, but not at all about what has happened to Gerald.

As a suspense novel *The Centurion* works reasonably well until the very end, which comes much too soon. Because we never meet the Centurion himself, we are unconvinced of his power. We can not gauge whether his interest is for political gain, the sheer megalomania of having produced chaos, or some other consuming value or passion. Without it the whole novel becomes something of a let-down. Even so, it is fun most of the way.

It is for his other two books, *A Lonely Place to Die* and *Divide the Night*, though, that Americans know Ebersohn best. They are, in addition, the closest to the traditional crime story of the author's oeuvre. Set in South Africa, they follow the work of James McClure and his fictional team of Kramer & Zondi. With an unlikely and somewhat eccentric protagonist, Prison Department Psychologist Yudel Gordon, however, they resemble not so much the traditional detective story as dramatic tales of conflict between Good and Evil, Black and White, and the confusion that surrounds them in the harsh social climate of Apartheid.

The first, *A Lonely Place to Die* (1979), begins at a party at the home of a landholder and Government minister, Marthinus Pretorius. When his son dies of poisoned mushrooms in the food, one of the Black workers, a retarded young man named Muskiet is imprisoned for the crime. Yudel is first brought into the case as an investigator, to establish Muskiet's sanity. Muskiet, he finds, is both deranged and deathly afraid, but does not have the cunning to think of all of the things needed to perform the murder.

In order to discover more, Gordon goes to the town. There he meets the dead man's sister Marie, their father the Minister, and Marie's lesbian lover Rebecca. He attends a Pentacostalist church service with Marie, and attempts to discover how this pretty young woman fits into the situation and what her place in the family structure is. The local police Lieutenant and his son, one of the sergeants, play roles of seeming helpfulness which barely hide their fury toward the outsider who presumes to know better than they. They hound him and taunt him as he tries to find complications where they insist none exist. Gordon's investigation also uncovers a small band of young white supremacists who counted young Marthinus among themselves.

Yudel's attempt brings him into contact also with Muskiet's mother, an old woman whose fear is great, but who also wishes to live in peace and not be bothered by the horrors which the Bosses have inflicted on her and her son. He also receives help from the Brothers at a monastery outside the town, especially Brother N'Kosana, whom he saves from murder at the hands of a band of young white thugs.

The novel ends when Gordon discovers the culprit for the murder of young Pretorius, and a long-standing pattern of behavior that led to it. When his friend, police Inspector Freek Jordan, who sent him to the town, picks him up at the end of the book, though, there is a final bit of ironic news. Muskiet, in a fit of passion, has killed a prison warder. The "convenience" of this final crime, keeping the schizophrenic in prison and away from his mother and help, seems to Yudel just another frustration in an irresolvable and ambiguous situation.

The second book featuring this attractive and complex man, *Divide the Night*, begins when a young, poor black girl enters a store late at night and is killed by the owner. The shopkeeper, Johnny Weizmann, is sent to Gordon at Freek Jordan's insistence for evaluation and possible treatment. The policeman is concerned, because Weizmann has been involved with the law several times over a period of years, and has killed and maimed several blacks, always claiming self-defense.

What Yudel finds when he meets Weizmann is a man entirely enveloped in fears from his childhood. In particular, Johnny exhibits a paralysis when, under hypnosis in Gordon's office, he is confronted by thoughts of his father, a man who beat him mercilessly. Unable to break through to ameliorate them, Gordon understands their power over Weizmann's life. In order to help the shopkeeper overcome these fears, Yudel suggests long-term therapy, which the other man adamantly refuses.

The story becomes more complex when Gordon and his wife are visited by the State Police, who inquire whether Weizmann is a patient. This leads Yudel to the case files of the man's earlier recorded cases. These turn out to be repeated confrontations which apparently set off a bloody response. More disturbing, the police have treated each case in isolation, believing Weizmann rather than his victims.

When Weizmann refuses to return for his third visit, Gordon visits his store, and then continues his investigation. He finds that a servant in a building across the street may have been a witness. She tells him that a strange black man was loitering near the scene, who may have also seen the young girl's death. Gordon further learns that the mysterious figure may be Mantu Majola, a wanted fugitive, a man banned and hunted for anti-state activities. Through his contacts with friends in the anti-government activist community, Yudel visits the Black Township of Soweto late at night, to tell the man's wife what he has discovered, and to elicit her help in resolving the situation. She is sympathetic, but will do nothing to assist him. When he returns to his friends' home he finds that the husband has been taken by the police. Later he receives a puzzling telephone call from the black woman, who has vanished.

After Gordon shows Freek Jordan what he has discovered about Weizmann's most recent crime, the two men attend a meeting of a virulent anti-government white group, of which Weizmann is a member. This makes vivid the ties between the lives of ordinary South Africans and the pervasive fear by many of them that white South Africa will be overwhelmed by the Blacks. After the meeting the pair are taken by a member of State Security to a jail compound, where they see both the man who made the contact for Yudel, and Majola's woman, whom Gordon met in the township, both under torture. He is horrified to realize that the police do not want to know the whereabouts of Muntu, but the name of the man who visited her several nights before—himself!

At home alone, as Gordon attempts to tie the things he knows to those he feels, he feels the presence of the black man he has been searching for. They talk, with Majola accusing Yudel of not caring, not taking a stand in previous outbreaks. After he leaves, Gordon calls Freek and they race to Johannesburg to stop Majola from killing Weizmann. In a dramatic conclusion, Freek kills Majola as he attempts to escape after attempting to assassinate Weizmann.

### III. Conclusion

All five of Wessel Ebersohn's novels (three have been released in the United States as of mid-1990) deal with the emotional quality that Evil releases in people. In his best evocations of it—the fanaticism of a Hitler or the banality of a South African policeman as he slowly tortures his victims until, seemingly without his realizing it, they slip over the edge into death—the writer makes clear that there is little if any appreciation by the perpetrators of the response they elicit. Nor do they care about the reasons for the responses of their victims, or of the onlookers whose horror stems both from the barbarity of the actions and from the nonchalance of the perpetrator. The work they do has been ordained, by powers beyond their ken and outside their control.

Ebersohn's most successful scenes have personalized these terrible forces, by taking the reader into the mind of his villains, showing the intensity of emotions. In this he has succeeded even better than his countryman James McClure. He is at his best in the torture chambers of *Divide the Night,* forcing both Yudel Gordon and the reader to confront the terrible reality that we know exists but cannot permit ourselves to acknowledge.

As a writer of psycho-social terror, Ebersohn achieves only moderate success. The power of the Evil Genius in *The Centurion* cannot be doubted, especially after the death of Gerald King's friend William Marshall. Yet because King never faces this villain, the well-created build-up is not satisfactorily concluded. The frightening conclusion is vitiated, rather than satisfied, by the reader's unfilled desire to meet the madman at the center of the plot, and to ask him "What is the meaning of all this?" The emptiness at the center of the web must be filled if the writer's original goal can be met.

# Chapter 11
# Spotlight on South Africa:
# The Police Novels of James McClure

**Eugene Schleh**

James Howe McClure was born in Johannesburg, South Africa October 9, 1939. After periods as a commercial photographer and as a teacher at a boys prep school, he moved to journalism as a reporter for several Natal newspapers from 1963 to 1965. In 1965 he moved to Great Britain and worked in editorial positions for several newspapers before turning to writing. Among the books he has published since 1971 is a series which centers on a unique pair of homicide detectives, Lieutenant Tromp Kramer and his assistant, Bantu Detective Sergeant Mickey Zondi. McClure has been quoted as saying that the primary aim of his writing is to entertain and in this he certainly succeeds and deserves the broad circulation he has achieved. His works, however, also fulfill a second purpose—they have quite a bit to say about the author's native land, past, present, and future.

Allen Drury once called South Africa "A Very Strange Society" and so it must appear to the average American. McClure's novels provide at least one man's insight into the workings of that society. They present not only examples of the way of life which makes international headlines, but, perhaps also, a message of hope.

Published in *Clues*, vol. 7, no. 2 (Fall/Winter 1986). Reprinted with permission.

*Text references are to pages in the novels listed by letter in the accompanying works cited.

Formal history is sparse in the novels. There is an occasional reference to the Boer War (B, 131)* or to Zulu troops serving in World War II as non-combatants (B, 91) and to the anti-Nationalist political activities of war hero Sailor Malan (F, 92). But these are not history books. More frequent are passing allusions to tid bits which suggest something about the society or changes to it. Afrikaans is labeled a new language with the word for "academic" only recently introduced (E, 34); television is belatedly accepted in South Africa (E, 76); the country becomes the world's largest distributor of complete Bibles in 1975 while the English-speaking press is already claiming world leadership in gun-owning, divorces, murders, assaults, road deaths, suicides, persons shot by the police, and executions (E, 55). It is indeed a Very Strange Society.

After more than two decades of official Apartheid it is impossible to write a novel of daily life in South Africa without some allusions to "the system." McClure's characters live in a segregated world whether it be the seating arrangements in court, a whites only telephone kiosk, or the need for all persons to carry the "Book of Life" registration documents. Major laws play their role with segregated housing being an unavoidable subject ranging from Zondi's home in a black township to changing a neighborhood from White to Coloured under the Group Areas Act (A, 148). Even wealthy Bantu businessmen can be endorsed out of an area and sent back to a Homeland (C, 80), pass offenders are rounded up, Black Spot evictions are carried out (D, 20). Laws keep most Bantu out of the towns overnight (A, 23), husbands have to visit wives who work as housemaids secretly and illegally (D, 168), and violation of the Immorality Act banning sex across race lines can ruin a man's life (A, 93) or even serve as a logical basis for a murder conspiracy (A).

Down to absurd levels, petty-Apartheid appears. Black school children are prevented from even standing in the rear of a whites-only museum cinema to see a nature film (D, 70) and at the police morgue even the dead bodies of Whites take precedence over those of non-Whites.

Underlying the formal legal system in South Africa is a puritanical religious system which must be understood. The Dutch Reformed Churches still hold strong influence among Afrikaners and their views of morality show up in daily life. Censorship, for example, is not solely of political material, but concerned with the evils of *Playboy* (A, 186) and photographic magazines (A, 86). As an innocent outlet a library saves censored books and passes them out to its staff as Christmas presents (C, 82). While some of the Afrikaner characters have doubts about the evil of miniskirts (A, 162), they seem to accept as normal banning women from bars (B, 8) and even an Orange Free State regulation keeping sunbathers 18 inches apart. Sundays are quiet in South Africa with curfews on Saturday ending drink and entertainment (D, 7) in time to leave the sabbath to the control of men like the police colonel who is a full church elder in a "black frock coat" (E, 45). This strain of thought and behavior is important to the Afrikaner nationalist for it is but another aspect of the belief that Afrikaners are a chosen people, "pure and divinely inspired" (B, 35).

These novels are not a mere retelling of familiar formal laws. Of much greater interest is their perspective on the thought processes of South Africans. Whites have deeply rooted views of Bantu mentality and these affect their daily behavior. A landlady dries her underwear indoors for fear that the sight of the garments would incite her garden boy (A, 99). In the morgue, the supervisor regularly chases away black attendants and police when a white woman's body is to be examined. Whites naturally mutter about "wog mentality" and just assume blacks starving to death is death by "natural causes" (B, 49).

Yet there are slight hints of change. Habits must be altered when "Kaffir" becomes a banned word (D, 57). Some, like the police colonel wince at the thought of soon having even "our little black friend Zondi" arresting white suspects (D, 163). A policeman watches a black woman using a homemade wheelbarrow to collect cardboard and cartons and thinks "It was true what they said: some of them were beginning to use brains instead of backsides" (D, 129). The winds or perhaps, at least, slight breezes or change blow even on Kramer when he interrogates a black physician: "Kramer was not used to having a wog address him in such a tone, still less to hearing one speak proper English and with an English accent, too. The sheer novelty won him over" (C, 136-137).

In South Africa there are four legal racial groups. Besides Whites and Blacks, the system is further complicated by sizeable numbers of Asians (mostly Indians) and Coloureds (those of mixed descent).

To McClure's whites all Asian males are "Sammy" and females "Mary" (B, 99) when they are not addressed with less polite terms like "coolie" or "curry guts." Durban is alien to Kramer, in some part because of so many Indians roaming around. The negative comparison of newcomer Portuguese refugees from Mozambique to Asians seems natural to a policeman who feels they are all running tearooms these days: "Worse then the coolies." (D, 39).

More mixed are white reactions to Coloureds. The latter may be close enough to whites to "pass" or even be formally reclassified. While killing a Coloured is "not quite the same" as killing a white (A, 189), there is evidence of some reevaluation. One policeman ruminates: "Many whites believe coloreds were a mixture of the worst characteristics of all the races whose blood ran in their veins; more often than not, Wessels had discovered, this was gross slander" (D, 116).

Indeed, by sheer volume of reactions and incidents, Kramer's antipathy is not directed at Asians, Coloreds, or Blacks. It is reserved for that generations old foe of the Afrikaner, the English. To Kramer, thinking of someone as "not bad for an English-speaking bloke" is a high compliment (A, 20). He finds English firemen (they seem to dominate that field as much as Afrikaners dominate the police) disrespectful (C, 148), is shocked that an Afrikaner boy has an English girlfriend (B, 97), has a "natural distrust of an Afrikaner with an English name" (C, 39). In the course of his work Kramer appears to meet a steady stream of English speakers who insult or at least slight Afrikaners and Afrikaans—admittedly he is very sensitive on these subjects. A drunken Englishman challenges Kramer's ability to understand a jest "in your bloody Dutch patois" and Kramer shows restraint in not responding to his "jibs at sixty percent of the white population" (B, 107). An Englishman finds it "remarkable" that Kramer should prefer Pernod to Cape brandy

(B, 131) and an English-speaking woman angrily charges that "You Afrikaans...You're as crude as my father always said." Kramer limits himself to smiling pleasantly while he replies "Afrikaans is a language, Miss Weston....I am an *Afrikaner*" (C, 60).

Kramer is fluent in English; he just doesn't like it. He insists that a young English-speaking policeman address him in Afrikaans (B, 120), knows the scandal mongering English-press "has its spies everywhere" (B, 76), and basically knows that "English was a dirty language at the best of times" (C, 91). His reactions are summed up in his following thoughts: "Names like Digby-Smith had always irritated Kramer. They smacked of English-speaking snobs with horse dung under their fingernails and—after drug-crazed alcoholic clap-struck half-castes—there was no breed of human he distrusted more profoundly" (F, 30).

The deepest insights can be gained by examining the two main characters and their relationship. The reader is not told a great deal about Kramer. He carries a 357 Ruger magnum, has no particularly unusual tastes, except, perhaps, his favorite breakfast of two jam doughnuts and a bottle of ginger beer (G, 16), and displays a mildly negative reaction to personnel or regulations which get in the way of his investigations—in short he comes over as a sort of Southern Hemisphere "Dirty Harry." Kramer has a long time romance with the Widow Fourie and obviously feels fairly strongly about her and her children. Since he spends little of his salary, he buys a house, Blue Haze, and rents it to her for what she had been paying for a flat and also makes her the recipient of the property in his will (D, 50). He himself is satisfied to live in a boarding house (F, 156).

Zondi's portrayal is more complex. He is clearly atypical for any society, much less South Africa's. Dressed in a zoot suit with glittering thread, he has a walk that is "pure Chicago," and his normal equipment includes a Walther PPK in its shoulder holster and two eight-inch knives held by elastic trouser tabs on either side (A, 32-32). Zondi has an excellent memory which he attributes to his mission school not being able to afford individual text books (B, 135). He is fluent in Zulu, Xosa, Sesutu, English, and Afrikaans to a degree which surprises some white policemen (F, 86: B, 126).

He joined the police early, after several years as a domestic servant, and moved up after meeting Kramer. Under Apartheid he lives simply for many years in an African township, Kwela Village, with his wife, Miriam, and their five children. They had only two rooms in a standardized Bantu house although Miriam had done her best to individualize it with trimmings like a pathway bordered by milk can tops, lines etched in the dirt floor to give it the appearance of boards, and newspapers to decorate kitchen shelves (C, 129-130; F, 105). Only by the most recent volume has Zondi been able to provide a still modest house which Miriam can be proud of in a new Bantu urban development eight miles outside of town. Now he can contemplate the arrival of electricity and, pending that, watch a small television set run off a car battery (G, 237-238).

Zondi is cautious and conservative. He worries about his children being exposed to agitators at school (E, 57), but also about the limits they will face as they grow older. He, himself, must know he is good, but he takes care not to rock the boat or assert himself. At one point he goes to buy his children an atlas as a reward for their school grades. A well meaning White salesclerk tries to talk him out of spending so much on a book which only contains maps and Zondi politely assures her with the fiction that he is buying it on orders from his White master (F, 206). At another point he is genuinely embarrassed when he receives an official commendation from his police superiors (F, 267). Again when an English girl Kramer is having an affair with wants Zondi to call her by her first name, he finds it unnatural and impossible.

How can such a system and the impact it has on even a skilled professional policeman be termed hopeful? Certainly developments elsewhere on the continent are not held up as an example (with the sole example of a reference to neighboring, desegregated Lesotho as a land of hope (A, 85). It is on the personal level, in the relationship between Kramer and Zondi that one may find a note of optimism. They are not socializing buddies who head off to a bar together after work. Indeed even on the job they comply openly with the expectations of a segregated society. In public Zondi walks a pace behind Kramer (F, 69) and Trompie, when speaking with White colleagues, refers to Zondi as an "idle Kaffir" (A, 22) or complains that "that Kaffir...does nothing but bloody sleep" (C, 175).

But this sort of thing is for public consumption. Alone the relationship is quite different. Kramer may have Zondi do "Kaffir work" by searching a garbage can (A, 34), but he would do the same with any White subordinate. The reality is that the two men like each other. They share cigarettes, laugh together often, exchange bantering insults, and trust their lives to each other. Their professional respect is solid, but it has also grown to something greater—deep personal respect and affection. When Zondi is injured in an auto accident and feared to be dying, Kramer tramples on the laws by driving the Widow and her children to Kwela Village to bring food, toys, and clothes to Zondi's family (C, 127). It is not just a gesture of charity. Kramer is hurt and fearful—concern that he shows at other times when Zondi is off along on a dangerous mission. Perhaps even Kramer himself is not fully aware of his subconscious feelings. Tish, his English girlfriend, tells him once that he has talked about Zondi a lot—in his sleep (F, 215).

That two men of such different cultures could find such deep respect and friendship is indeed hopeful. In the face of such relationships the significance of laws can be lessened and the laws themselves can crumble away. The process, however, is slow and evolutionary. Whether enough time remains for Kramer and Zondi to be symbolic of a new South Africa remains to be seen.

# Works Cited

## Novels of James McClure
## (editions used for this paper)

A   *The Steam Pig.* New York: Harper & Row, Publishers, 1971.
B   *The Caterpillar Cop.* New York: Pantheon Books, 1972.
C   *The Gooseberry Fool.* Harmondsworth, U.K.: Penguin Books, 1974.
D   *Snake.* New York: Avon Books, 1976.
E   *The Sunday Hangman.* New York: Avon Books, 1977.
F   *The Blood of an Englishman.* New York: Pantheon Books, 1980.

# Chapter 12
## Interview with James McClure
## Headington, England
## October 27-28, 1988

(**W** = Don Wall          Mc = James McClure)

**W:** You refer to your Kramer and Zondi books as "crime fiction" rather than as "mysteries," although the books are built around mysteries to be solved. What does this distinction mean to you?

**Mc:** I think the distinction is simply between what this type of book is called in England and America, because here we have a Crime Writers Association and in America you have the Mystery Writers of America. It's the difference between "boot" and "trunk" in a motor car—or automobile—that's all. On top of which, though, "mysteries" always sounds to me somewhat superficial, and I prefer to call it crime writing because principally I write about crime, about societies. "Mystery" I think underscores the *contrived* element in crime writing—that we always have solutions, a parlour game. The kind of crime writing that I try to do, and that I like to read, is concerned with real, or near-real, life and consequences. I find "mystery" trivializes. I certainly never set out to write a mystery. As somebody once said, it's the journey, not the destination, that matters. If somebody set off to discover the source of the White Nile, which to a degree *is* a mystery, it's the journey there that's the interesting part, really. And I think almost inevitably, no matter how clever, the solution is where the tension of a story breaks.

**W:** Yes, but why *crime*? Why not "straight" novels, so to speak?

**Mc:** I'd be quite happy if my books weren't called crime novels. Often the crime is virtually irrelevant. More important are the people you meet—even people who aren't part of the direct evidence, so to speak. There's a sequence in *The Artful Egg* where Kramer goes to a boardinghouse and the woman answers every question with a single word. It's the experience of meeting *her*—that's the value of that scene.

Why did I choose this so-called genre? Because crime is something I knew quite a lot about, and again, because I wanted to write about South Africa in a context which would allow South Africa to become incidental to the story. Which doesn't mean it isn't very much *part* of the story. Unlike some other writers about South Africa, I try to make sure that the action is *peculiar* to that environment and arises out of it.

Some South African crime novels are just absurd. The last one I read, the plot could equally have been written in Florida or any damned place. It wasn't particularly South African, mainly ludicrous and spuriously "liberal" in its politics.

Then again, I chose this genre also because it allowed me to reach a much greater audience than it would if I wrote about South Africa in a straight novel. That way, you preach to nobody but the converted, usually—or to the so-called intellectual reader. You're not reaching the ordinary guy at all. I think one of the weirdest pieces of fan mail I ever got was from a Reno divorce hotel, where the guy just said, "Trekkersburg is Pietermaritzburg, right?" People of all kinds read my stuff, and that is really important to me.

Also, it's a genre which allows a great social mobility. It's difficult in an ordinary novel, unless you're perhaps writing about doctors or something, to travel constantly from one social level to another. But even with doctors you cannot combine races and languages that easily—you don't get doctors or surgeons with black sidekicks. So it gives you access—opens the whole scene up. Here the mystery is a great help because that's what the audience is basically concerned with, that's where the main thread is, and it's apolitical in itself. How much else readers pick up is up to them, and I think that's much fairer. It's astonishing how varied are the reactions you'll get to the same Kramer and Zondi story. You'll get a South African review saying it's very realistic and they love it very much and they see nothing in it even vaguely subversive, and then you get *The Times* of London, "Hey, buddy, you read this stuff and anybody who can't see it is subversive is a fool."

If you write a straight novel about South Africa, it's impossible, really, not to make it a political novel—and as soon as it's a political novel, it has to *stand* somewhere. A so-called "mystery" has far greater independence, the same book can contain many types of politics—and I think the *experience* of the country is far more important than anything else. It's the function of a novel to deal in experience and feeling, and argument—political argument—has no business in it. Nearly every novel I've ever read about South Africa becomes a political argument, where the people become secondary to the political argument. That's not my idea of reality.

**W:** A basic truth is that novels should be entertaining—I doubt that any writer starts out thinking, "I'm going to bore the socks off as many people as I can"—so let's start with the assumption that writers aim to tell a good, interesting story. Novels which do that have a chance of becoming, and remaining, popular. Certainly your novels satisfy this criterion.

Also, you take some pride in getting things right, getting things down *accurately*, which accounts in large measure for their popularity among South Africans. You have mentioned that this is one of the main reasons the South African Police like them, for example.

But you have been away from South Africa for quite a few years now, and conditions in some ways have changed so much that, in a sense, your Kramer-and-Zondi's can be thought of as historical novels.

Assuming that people can learn from history, what do you think intelligent, thoughtful readers can still learn from the Kramer and Zondi novels?

**Mc:** Kramer-and-Zondi books are indeed historical novels, inasmuch as they give us some idea about what created the present situation.

Yet the essential things in them are probably no different, however much things have changed in the country at one level.

**W:** Like what?

**Mc:** Well, despite everything, despite the divisions and all the rest of it, there are strong friendships and relationships formed across barriers of race—not only in the case of Kramer and Zondi. In *Snake* there's a clear example of that where the real mother of somebody turns out in real terms to be the black nanny.

I'm pretty sure that kind of stuff isn't going to change—isn't likely to change. I'd also expect that another of the things that isn't going to change is the sheer complexity of the nuances of life in South Africa.

**W:** A somewhat related question is this: What do your books reveal about South Africa that other South African writers whose work you know does not?

**Mc:** I can't very well reply to this question as I don't really know the work of any other South African writer. I've read so very little because I'm seldom entertained by it and find it fearfully predictable.

**W:** You've read Alan Paton, Nadine Gordimer.

**Mc:** And my reaction is, where is the humor in it? It's all as deadly serious as a political meeting. I always hear laughter as well as sobbing when I recall life in Africa.

**W:** Is that why you like Bosman?

**Mc:** Yes, I think that Herman Charles Bosman was, at his best, a far superior writer.

**W:** What does he capture about Africa that attracts you to him?

**Mc:** I think that he has *affection* for everybody he writes about. Despite the fact he's enormously acerbic, and, if you like, incisive and cutting, and sees them for what they are, this is very real affection.

**W:** But that's you, too, isn't it? Don't you also have an affection for the people you write about?

**Mc:** Yes, I do, and that's a word that keeps being repeated in South African reviews of my books.

**W:** What, affection?

**Mc:** "Clearly loves the people he writes about," and so forth. Perhaps this goes somewhere to explain one of the lesser mysteries of these mystery books, which is that none of them have been banned, except the one that contained banned material, which very naturally would have to be banned—*The Sunday Hangman*. It dealt with South African prisons and with hanging, and with other things that come under the Prisons Act, which forbids anything being written about these matters. So I didn't ever expect that one to slide through. If you look at the *content* of the other books, there's plenty in them to offend if removed from its context, but *in* context, it causes no offense, alarm, or whatever. South Africans find it "the way things are." Other people read it, share this experience of South Africa, and condemn it—just as they would if most of those readers went and stayed in South Africa for a while. I have always felt that if a truth exists, you don't have to argue it. You just put it down—people aren't so dumb they can't make up their own minds about it.

Another reason I've chosen to write in a crime milieu goes back to when I took a group of children I was teaching, lads about eleven years old, to a performance of *MacBeth* at the university. That wasn't the world's greatest performance, but it was a very spirited affair, and these kids really enjoyed it: they enjoyed the witches, enjoyed the ghost, enjoyed the bloodletting, they enjoyed the crazy lady—enjoyed the rude stuff the porter said—everything. What they were actually enjoying was almost a comic book level of that play—the violence and naughty words and scarey bits and all that. And sitting opposite them on the other side of this round stage which is in the center of the amphitheater was a bunch of real heavy Englit students, and they were *also* enjoying it, at a different level—plus probably that first level as well. I always believe in a first level. And there was a man I had a great deal of regard for, a Professor of English, and he was drawing *his* own pleasure from it.

To my mind, a real—if you like—work of art is something that can hit at all levels. Whereas I feel that a lot of books about South Africa are only going to appeal at one, maybe two levels. Perhaps the argument level, with a bit of emotion thrown in. *Perhaps my books*—I must say perhaps—reveal more about South Africa because they range across a tremendous number of layers of South African society, from the poor and illiterate black, to the intelligent, literate, successful, professional black, and again, with the two white tribes, they also include things which are barbaric and savage and African. I do not mean black African, I mean *of Africa*, which is not necessarily black. I believe Africa has its own character, perhaps in many ways not very different to Ireland or Scotland not very long ago. If you read the history of the Highlands of Scotland, when they used to roar about in plaids and whack each other with swords and steal each other's cattle, they sound exactly like 19th century Zulus. And in fact the Scots and the Zulus have a great deal in common in that they are both a very military, militant race. Some of the finest regiments are Scottish regiments, with their great absurdities like the bagpipe player who marches in the front, unarmed, except for this fearful sound. And that's very like the sort of thing the Zulus did, as well. I sometimes think that heightens aspects of my Zulu nature.

Oh aye, I've got a lot of Zulu in me. I didn't become aware of this until I was watching *Wousa Albert*, a play staged by two black South Africans who brought it to London. A friend of mine said, "My God, I see where you get it from," because I apparently used certain fixed gestures, which indeed were Zulu gestures, and I also used sound effects when I spoke, again without being conscious of this.

I also feel I've experienced greater conflicts than the other South Africans writers I've come across. I cannot think of one of them whose life hasn't run along the lines of an academic start, and what contact they make with people, Afrikaner and black, has probably been fairly formal, in a sense—you know, poetry workshops, intelligent parties with lots of intelligent red wine. I don't think, from what I can make out, they've had much experience of South Africa in the raw.

**W:** Is this true of Paton, too?

**Mc:** Yes. Yes, I don't think Paton has had much experience of these things at all. As a personality, he was a very aggressive man. He smoldered and snapped. He ran, for a considerable length of time, a reformatory for black delinquents, and allowed his children to amuse themselves by marching the delinquents about. As a matter of fact, I can't see Paton mixing readily in *any* company—no true breadth of experience. I'm not saying my books are necessarily better, but I don't find their books about South Africa half as bloody complicated as I find South Africa. Mary Benson, for example, wrote a novel in which her black security policemen were all monsters. But I *know* they're *not* all monsters—far from it. What fascinates me is the man who isn't a monster who works as a monster. I find that much more interesting than monsters. There's no *insight* into these people—a form of literary apartheid.

Something that was really quite indicative of the attitude of so many white liberals occurred when an aborted attempt was made at filming *The Steam Pig* [in Pietermaritzburg], and John Khani, a Xhosa actor who'd won top awards on Broadway and in London for his roles in plays that were shattering condemnations of the South African political scene, was playing the part of Zondi. Time and again John would be asked by white "liberals" how he could bring himself to play the part of a black detective in the South African police force? He would tell them it wasn't that difficult, because that's what his father had been—and he had been a good man.

I can't stand stereotyping, and a lot of the things I've read by South African novelists about South Africa are as repulsive to me as the outright fascism and racialism of the more rabid Nationalist Party member, because they're equally prone to stereotype.

**W:** You've partially answered my last question, which is that people—*I* think—have oversimplified your view of apartheid. You're not an apologist for it and you certainly don't defend it, it's an abhorrent policy to you, but, on the other hand, you understand the people who live under that system, and you see that good men can live under a bad policy and do *good* things, too.

**Mc:** Yes.

**W:** Is that stating it accurately? For instance, I think Kramer is a good example. He's not a liberal, but he's a kind of person who can recognize and appreciate individual human beings for their worth. There's that wonderful scene in *The Artful Egg* where the white driver swipes a paper from the Indian newsboy, and Kramer pulls him over and handcuffs him to his steering wheel. It's almost a peripheral thing on Kramer's part. He's concerned with other things at the time, he sees that, it pisses him off, and he pulls the guy over, he humbles him, and then he's off.

**Mc:** That is the finest example you could have chosen, but let me tell you a parable.

Back when I was a crime reporter in South Africa, there was a guy I met called, let's say, Boet Boerman, a Murder and Robbery Squad detective sergeant. At night the C.I.D. building used to be empty and dark except for the Murder and Robbery office, most of the time. Boet would sit in there and wait for calls and I used to sit on his desk, and he would tell me things about his life. I realized very quickly that he was talking about the world of Herman Charles Bosman, who wrote a marvelous book called *Mafeking Road*, a series of short stories about people living in a very dry area near what is now Namibia. Boet had never heard of Bosman, the irony being this great South African writer was an Afrikaner but he'd been brought up at a time when Afrikaans was not taught to Afrikaners so he'd written in English. I lent Boet this collection of stories and he was delighted with them. It was the first book he'd ever read that was not a manual of some sort. And the irony was that he'd tell me parallel stories of his life and beginnings. His story emerged in bits and pieces and patches because we never talked for long, but I'm going to put it back in chronological order.

First, I'm going to tell you a little bit about what I knew about the man who sat opposite me. He was a very personable young man, about twenty-seven. He looked like a successful young executive. He had a very relaxed manner. He wore a very neat suit and a neat tie. He looked like he worked in a bank.

And I knew, because I'd been up there, that he lived in a really nice little ranch house, as we call it, up in a valley, with a couple of garages, two cars, nice kids, nice wife; he was comfortable.

And he sat opposite me at his desk, with his Walther PPK and his shoulder holster. But he was not a macho guy, in the demonstrative sense. Now at any moment he could be called out to a murder, and probably face a great deal of danger. But he was not a man to make a fuss about this.

And now to go back to his story. He told me he'd been born in this hamlet called_____. The land was so poor that the government, to keep the farmers earning anything, sent by train enormous numbers of grapes, which these farmers then spread out under the sun and turned into raisins.

Every morning four wagons travelled into the village from the four points of the compass, carrying the kids to school. It was run by a man called "Die Meester," "The Master." That isn't the Afrikaans word for a teacher, which is "onderwyser." "Die Meester" carries a much more awesome connotation. It reminded me of what I'd read in *Esquire* about sharecroppers, in that all these farmers were in constant debt to Die Meester because he not only ran the school, but also the only store.

The greatest thing in Boet's life was that every two weeks a policeman rode into the village—it was such a quiet neighborhood, that's all they ever saw the cops. Boet couldn't believe this guy— he had this fantastic horse. Boet's father had no horse, he was too poor. Moreover, this policeman had these wonderful shiny leather leggings. Boet had never seen anything quite like them.

There were a lot of little black kids hanging around, and they would rush to hold this policeman's horse for the tip. But Boet would beat them aside, because *he* wanted to hold those reins, so that he would have a long look at the horse. The policeman would then go into the schoolhouse and drink coffee with Die Meester for an hour or so, to find out what was happening locally.

One afternoon the policeman came out and said to Boet, "Why do you fight the kaffirs to hold my horse?" So he told him how much he liked the horse and his leggings. "Would *you* like leggings just like these?" the cop asked, and Boet said, "Yes, very much!" And he would like a horse, too.

"How old are you?" asked the cop.

"I'm fifteen," said Boet.

"Well, next year you can have these things," the policeman told him.

Boet could hardly contain himself, even when the policeman also told him he had to have his standard six exam—which you reach after eight years at school, which is not a lot.

Boet worked very hard, passed his exam, and the time came for him to go to the police college. And so, they made him a bundle— *not* a suitcase, they did not *own* a suitcase. And true enough, the policeman came, and he had a second horse. He put Boet on it and he clung to it for dear life. They had to tie the bundle separately, because he had no hands for that. They didn't go as far as Boet expected. They came to a railway line in the desert, and the policeman said, "Just get off your horse and wait here." After a while a train appeared in the distance. The policeman just held up his hand and the train stopped—he'd arranged this before. Boet was put aboard the train and traveled to Pretoria, the Republic's administrative capital. He was then taken to the police training college, Voortrekkerhoogte.

Boet said, "Ach, I'll never forget the first night." Everyone had laughed at him, because when they had stew for their supper, he picked up a spoon and began to eat. The other recruits said, "Why don't you use your fork?" Well, they'd never had forks on Boet's table at home, just spoons. They were very poor.

He said there were a lot of shocks. He'd never heard a radio—it'd made him jump. He'd never read a newspaper. He'd seen der Meester with this thing, but didn't realize there was one of them every day, with all those words. And he was supposed to read this thing, and it took him bloody *hours.*

I said, "What about the bioscope?"—which is a South African term for the cinema.

Boet said, "Ach, that was a shock!" He'd never *seen* a bloody cow so big! And it was *noisy!*

The film was about the Mau Mau and began with this cow that's had its Achilles tendon slashed by Mau Mau pangas. The film scared the shit out of him—he decided that the Mau Mau were real bad asses. He saw a film about communists the same afternoon. He was sixteen, a very formative age. You only had to say "communist" to this guy and he would grow cold, cold, cold.

Yet Boet was a really nice man. I remember that I never once saw him hit a prisoner, and he would certainly have hit him in front of me, because other people were hitting them in front of me. And he was Mr. Straight Arrow. He solved a particularly atrocious murder in town, when a white shot a coloured man and dragged him into a yard and pretended he'd been trying to burgle the place. In reality, the coloured man had been there to protest the fact that the white was sleeping with his fiancee. It was Boet who solved the case and arrested the white, despite threats from the man's family.

But can you imagine the *impact* those first months in a conditioned atmosphere must have had on him? And yet there he is, urbane, pleasant, looking like a bank official—*until* you said "communist." And then, it threatened everything—his ranch house, his nice wife, his nice kids—even his nice servants, I guess you could say, because he was a very compassionate employer.

These guys who worked Murder and Robbery at night came and went, so he vanished for a while and I didn't think anything of it. I didn't see him around for a while, and then I was going down to court and Boet was walking ahead of me. I said I hadn't seen him around and he said, no, he'd changed jobs. He was in the Security Branch—he'd been picked for it.

And I knew that, in due course, when he arrested a friend of mine, he was a lot tougher on him than he'd ever been on a murder suspect. But even then he still didn't go over the top. Now there was no way I could ever hate Boet—no way. It comes down to that old Catholic saying: hate the song but not the singer.

My experience with so many men in the South African Police is akin to that.

I once had a friend, a witness in a bombing case with political overtones, who was given the third degree by the SB. He told me that what diverted him while this was going on was a Major who was one of the most notorious of all the interrogators—a man with an enormously brutal face.

This Major's mother used to phone, and he'd say, "Ja Mom? Of *course* I've got my jersey on, I *know* it's got cold tonight." And then he'd go back to interrogating him and knocking him about. The phone would ring: "Ja Ma? I'll have my sandwiches later. Yes, I've got the flask, don't worry, I've brought it with me," and put the phone down.

I'd like to tell some of those South African novelists that I've read that I wish *sometimes* the mothers would phone and ask if *their* cops had their jerseys on.

I just don't believe in stereotypes.

A long answer, Mr. Wall!

**W:** But a very intriguing one. Thank you!

# Contributors

**Earl F. Bargainnier** was Fuller E. Callaway Professor of English at Wesleyan College. A former President of the Popular Culture Association, he was the author of more than sixty articles and *The Gentle Art of Murder: The Detective Fiction of Agatha Christie.* He has previously edited *Ten Women of Mystery* and *Twelve Englishmen of Mystery* and co-edited *Cops and Constables.* Professor Bargainnier died January 3, 1987.

**Steven R. Carter** is Associate Professor at The University of Puerto Rico, specializing in African American, African, and Caribbean Literature. He has published more than thirty essays in these fields plus detective fiction and science fiction, and his book *Hansberry's Drama: Commitment Amid Complexity* will be published by The University of Illinois Press in February 1991.

**Fred Isaac** is currently Head Librarian at the Jewish Community Library in San Francisco. He has contributed essays to other Popular Press anthologies and has written book reviews and articles on numerous aspects of Detective fiction.

**Mary Lou Quinn** teaches history at Gray-New Gloucester High School in Gray, ME.

**Dieter Riegel** is Professor of German at Bishop's University in Lennoxville, Québec, Canada. His research interests include German crime fiction, workers' literature, and modern Danish literature.

**Sharon Russell** is Professor of Communication at Indiana State University. She has published articles on aspects of the mystery and horror genres in literature and film and is editing a collection on animals in mysteries for the Popular Press.

**Eugene Schleh** is a Professor of History at the University of Southern Maine.

**Don Wall** is Professor of English at Eastern Washington University, where he teaches courses in crime fiction and true crime cases. Currently he is President of the Northern Pacific Popular Culture Association and a Vice President of PCA. He has published articles on crime fiction, several mystery stories, and a Young Adult Soccer novel.